THEATRE AND STAGE SERIES

General Editor: HAROLD DOWNS

PROBLEMS OF ACTING
AND
PLAY PRODUCTION

PITMAN'S THEATRE AND STAGE SERIES

Edwin C. White

Fr.

PROBLEMS OF ACTING
AND
PLAY PRODUCTION

BY

EDWIN C. WHITE

WITH A FOREWORD BY

DAME FLORA ROBSON

LONDON

SIR ISAAC PITMAN & SONS LTD

First published 1939
Reprinted 1946
Revised and reprinted 1955
Reprinted 1957
Reprinted 1961
Reprinted 1966

SIR ISAAC PITMAN AND SONS LTD
Pitman House, Parker Street, Kingsway, London WC2
The Pitman Press, Bath
Pitman House, Bouverie Street, Carlton, Melbourne
20–25 Beckett's Buildings, President Street, Johannesburg

Associated Companies

PITMAN MEDICAL PUBLISHING COMPANY LTD
46 Charlotte Street, London WI

PITMAN PUBLISHING CORPORATION
20 East 46th Street, New York, N.Y. 10017

SIR ISAAC PITMAN (CANADA) LTD
Pitman House, 381–383 Church Street, Toronto

MADE IN GREAT BRITAIN AT THE PITMAN PRESS, BATH
F6—(G.137)

FOREWORD

THAT there are two sides to every question is a truism from which something can be gleaned. The dawn of naturalism in the theatre was also the beginning of refinement in play writing, in play production, in play interpretation. There was movement, and it was in the direction of refinement, by which I mean processes which in action made for the rounding of sharp corners, for the clarification of thought in relation to play writing, and for intelligence and imagination in interpretation. But these refining processes, while registering, on the whole, progress in the arts of the theatre, have also created dangers rather than difficulties. There is in my own profession the danger of under-acting in order to avoid the allegations that the technique of modern acting has not been mastered, that the "ham" acting of an obsolete age is persisting, and that the persistence strikes an incongruous note. The danger has not been avoided in some quarters. Indeed, it has been deliberately courted. There are well-informed, clever, artistic workers in the theatre who, believing in change, precipitate change by too rigorously applying new methods, to the exclusion of old methods, before conviction that the newer methods are improvements or progressive is firmly founded.

"How many times when one has been watching the performance of a naturalistic action," as I have written elsewhere, "has one heard a member of the audience say, 'But that is not acting, he is just being himself'! This may be a tribute to the actor's particular style, but it is not a true statement; he is, in reality, giving a highly finished performance, every movement and intonation of which is thought out to the last detail.

"The most important fact to make clear is that the actor is never being spontaneous or natural; he only *appears* to be."

This belief in the efficacy of being "oneself" is misleading, especially to the inexperienced or the uninitiated. To appear to be behaving naturally is often to demonstrate acting in some of its higher branches. Alas! appearances, even among members of the acting profession, have in some cases depreciated standards of interpretation—hence the pertinence of much that Mr. Edwin C. White, the author of this volume of challenge and of construction, states in terms of problems for which he himself, drawing upon a long and intimate experience of stage work of a specialized character, supplies solutions.

"Behaving is not acting. Yet to-day, on the professional as well as on the amateur stage," he states, "many actors are capable of doing little more than behaving as they do in their normal lives. This is partly due, perhaps, to a misconception of the purpose of the art of acting, and to a definite belief in naturalism and realism in art. But it is more often due, I feel, to the fact that actors are unaware of any other way."

Study is, undoubtedly, an essential, but study is not enough. With it must be allied patience, enterprise, imagination. The would-be player who is hoping to be a successful interpreter must be prepared to face much trouble and must be determined to overcome it. To read a part is not to understand it. Without understanding, the most polished performance will lack verisimilitude. There is, too, something to be learned about relationships. The author, to enforce some of his points, goes to the world of music. It supplies him with useful illustrations. The successful orchestral player is one of a team. The principal player in the cast, just as surely as the small-part player, is also one of a team. The relationship of part to part must be seen and acted *upon* so that it is acted *into* the interpretation of the play. Mastering lines will not suffice. There must be sensitiveness to the music of spoken speech. There must be observation to deepen understanding, which must be related not only to the physical but also to the mental states of the character portrayed. As I said elsewhere, a part should be conceived objectively and played subjectively. One of the most important attributes in naturalistic acting is that of seeming to be unconscious of anybody watching or listening. In intimate scenes this gives members of the audience the feeling that they are listening to people who have been left alone together.

The last thing a great actor acquires is ease. There never seems to be any strain about his performance: immense hard work goes before it, and then—through great control—comes ease. Beginners, watching this appearance of ease, want to imitate it, without realizing the work that must be done first in order to acquire it. In the same way players from small tennis clubs will try to imitate a Wimbledon player—always with disastrous results to their own game.

It would be easy to enumerate many other points that are of importance and that are really the raw materials upon which the artist draws in order to create the perfect portrayal. Mr. White works systematically through the player's armoury. The voice is important; so, too, are movement and gesture, perception of artistic requirements, of aspects of interpretative skill, without which no would-be artist can translate ideal into practice. He writes neither abstrusely nor pedantically, but clearly and pointedly, to "assist the student to gain skill in the mechanical details of the technique of acting, and also to establish certain principles governing the task of interpretation and communication of character." He has written, in short, a helpful volume that sacrifices nothing of genuine interest in presenting and emphasizing everything that is practical and related to the art of acting.

FLORA ROBSON

ACKNOWLEDGMENTS

For permission to include copyright matter I have been indepted to the following—

Miss Rosamond Gilder and Methuen & Co., Ltd., for passages from *John Gielgud's Hamlet*.
W. B. Yeats and Macmillan & Co., Ltd., for lines from *The Only Jealousy of Emer*.
Victor Gollancz, Ltd., for passages from *Children in Uniform*.
Mr. E. Lightly for curtain design of Lob's Wood (*Dear Brutus*).

E. C. W.

PUBLISHER'S NOTE

Since this book was first published it has become usual on the West End Stage, following American practice, to refer to the "producer" as "director." As this change in nomenclature has not yet been universally adopted, references to the "producer" have been left unaltered for the present reprint.

CONTENTS

ILLUSTRATIONS

INTRODUCTION

A COMMON practice of those interested in acting is to join a society established for the purpose of producing plays and to accept any part offered. This is undoubtedly one way of getting some fun and amusement, and perhaps of gaining a little experience in the art of acting. But I have often wondered what the conductor of an orchestra would say to the aspiring members of his orchestra if they came to him with no other qualification than the desire to play an instrument.

Most praiseworthy is the ambition to play an instrument in an orchestra, but before such can be realized a certain minimum of musical attainment is an admitted essential. Most laudable is the desire to interpret a part in a play, but rarely do we find anybody thinking that there is any necessity on the part of the would-be actor to qualify himself for the task in any way whatever. It would seem that there is a general belief that anybody who is able to read must be ready for the task of interpretation on the stage. I do not pretend to know how this belief has gained credence. I am merely aware that practice illustrates that it is a generally accepted truth.

Behaving is not acting. Yet to-day, on the professional as well as on the amateur stage, many actors are capable of doing little more than behaving as they do in their normal lives. This is partly due, perhaps, to a misconception of the purpose of the art of acting, and to a definite belief in naturalism and realism in art. But it is more often due, I feel, to the fact that actors are unaware of any other way of performing their task. They can only talk and walk and move as they do in their normal surroundings because they have neither considered nor practised any other way.

It is very probable that the Archbishop of Canterbury knows more about the behaviour of Thomas à Becket than does Mr. Robert Speaight, but it is very doubtful if the Archbishop would be able to give as full an interpretation of that character as does the actor. The knowledge of how to behave and the ability to behave are not the only qualities demanded of the actor. It is equally necessary for him to possess the ability to communicate his purposes to an audience in a theatre.

This condition imposes upon all who would act the necessity of acquiring skill in the very definite tasks that every actor will be called upon to perform. He must study the requirements of the stage, and he must practise so that he may gain ability to perform. The purpose of this book is to outline a method of study which will prepare the actor for his work on the stage. Its aim is to assist the student of acting to discover and develop a technique of his own. It is hoped that, by the study of exercises in speech, movement, and gesture, the student will be able to acquire the skill which is an essential condition for the interpretation of character in a theatre.

The exercises suggested are planned, firstly, to assist the student to gain skill in the mechanical details of the technique of acting, and, secondly, to establish certain principles governing the task of interpretation and communication of character. The examples taken for study and analysis are generally plays that are well known and readily accessible to the average reader. I have deliberately concentrated attention upon certain plays, because my chief purpose has been to focus thought upon details of technique and principles of interpretation.

At the end of each chapter I have set a number of exercises which should provide opportunity for applying knowledge and for gaining further experience. These exercises have been selected from a considerable variety of plays, both classical and modern.

In addition to problems of acting, I have also considered at some length some of the problems of play production. In this section of the book I have concentrated upon the problems of setting a stage, movement, and grouping of characters, as well as upon the very important task of working towards, and focusing attention upon, the climax of a play.

Throughout it has been my purpose to put forward practical and constructive suggestions which will be of service to those wishing to prepare themselves for the stage, either as actors or producers. As in all other arts, the joy in acting increases as skill is acquired and ability to interpret is realized. But ability will not come for the mere asking. Achievement will come through effort; joy will be found in striving to attain.

Finally, I must express my indebtedness and gratitude to my good friends Thomas Beach and Douglas Smith for their help and encouragement, and especially to Mr. Harold Downs for his sound, expert advice and willing help in every stage of the preparation of this book.

EDWIN C. WHITE

CHAPTER I

You Must Have a Purpose

YOU wish to act? Then you shall. You and your friend shall act a little play for my pleasure. Do not shirk the effort; it is very important that you should make it, because, remember, you wish to act.

The little play you are asked to perform is this—

The curtain goes up. You are sitting on one side of a table. Your friend is sitting on the other side. You sit, and sit, and sit. . . . The curtain comes down.

Get up on the stage and perform this play. It may last just as long as you wish.

Now you have tried to perform it, you will perhaps say—as so many others have said after their first efforts to act this little play—that you felt awkward and uncomfortable, that you didn't know what to do, or that the play was silly, or, more truthfully, that you felt silly. If you are able to watch others performing, you will observe that they too are uncomfortable, that one fidgets with his legs, that another looks coyly down at the carpet, that another looks affectedly towards his audience, while yet another sniggers at the very thought of being asked to do such a silly thing. What seemed to be a simple play did in fact become difficult because you had no *purpose* in doing anything at all on the stage.

Now take down your copy of Barrie's *Dear Brutus*. Turn to Act I, and about three-quarters of the way through you will find this speech of Mrs. Alice Dearth—

Miss Trout and I will await your return with ill-concealed impatience.

And now Alice and Joanna are left on the stage in just such a way as I have suggested you should sit in the exercise. They are sitting, one on either side of the table, waiting. Alice, in a reverie, is sitting, and Joanna is watching her.

If you read the subsequent dialogue, you will readily observe that each has a purpose in waiting there. Of what are they thinking? Alice is probably thinking of her pending interview with her husband, and the dialogue clearly indicates the attitude and thoughts of Joanna. Read this episode again and again until your mind can follow the rapid sequence of thoughts passing through the mind of Alice, her changing moods, and the subtlety with which she succeeds in getting rid of Joanna. Think of Joanna, of what has preceded this episode, and try to get at her thoughts as she sits looking at this woman who has intruded and interrupted a most interesting and romantic situation.

Barrie has created for each of these characters a very definite purpose for being on the stage. You also must have a clearly defined purpose for sitting on the stage.

Now repeat the scene yourself, and this time provide yourself with a purpose. If you like, let your purpose be similar to that of Alice and of Joanna. This time you will feel more comfortable, less self-conscious, but even now perhaps the audience will not follow the train of your thoughts. This will be because you have not the ability to *communicate your purpose* to an audience "across the footlights." In acting there is always this dual problem: the problem of interpreting and that of communicating. But we cannot hope, with our first step, to achieve the highest peaks of an art, so let us here concentrate upon having a purpose while we are on the stage, and perhaps we shall, with practice, achieve the ability to communicate this purpose as we progress in our study.

Now try another play—

The curtain goes up. You are sitting on the stage alone reading a book. The passage interests you. You pause to think about the passage. You resume reading. The curtain comes down.

In this exercise you are provided with action, but your imagination must supply *purpose* to your interpretation. The passage may be one that puzzles you, it may be one that amuses you, or it may be interesting because it recalls an incident from the past. Act this little play, keeping in mind your special purpose, and try so to act that your purpose may be communicated to your audience.

Here is another play for you to study and to act—

The curtain goes up. You are sitting on the stage expecting a visitor. You think you hear footsteps. No, you are mistaken. After a time you do hear footsteps, but just as you are expecting to hear a knock on the door, the footsteps pass on and beyond hearing. The curtain comes down.

Give your imagination rein as you construct a purpose for your interpretation of the scene. Are you expecting your lover, or is it someone you would rather not see? Is your anticipation one of pleasure, or will you be relieved if the expected visitor does not come? How will you show to your audience that it is your lover you are expecting? What will you do to indicate that you think you can hear footsteps? How will you show that you have been mistaken? Visualize the sequence of events and the progress of the thoughts passing through your mind. Let each thought and action lead naturally to each subsequent one, and be sure that everything you do on the stage has a definite purpose. Within the framework of this little play you may construct a most interesting little plot, and if you will be careful enough to ensure that everything—each look, each movement, each glance, and each simple gesture—has a definite purpose, you will perhaps be able to convey your plot to your audience.

These little plays are simple exercises, but the interpretation of each demands a certain skill. That skill is acting. You can acquire that skill by thought and practice—by thinking out your purpose, and by practising movements and gestures and facial expressions to convey your purpose to an audience.

The second exercise, very much extended and elaborated, represents a scene from *The Great Lover*, a scene in which Maurice Moscovitch revealed his great artistic skill when this play was produced at the Shaftesbury Theatre some years ago. In this scene he silently read a number of letters from old lovers. From his chuckles of delight, from the sad expression of his eyes, and from the slow and staring expression of his gaze we could follow his thoughts and construct in imagination something of his past love affairs. There was purpose in everything he did. He read slowly; he read rapidly; sometimes passages were read over again; sometimes he would pause, and from his expression we knew that memory was painful; sometimes he would fling a letter from him; and at other times he would linger over the pages and cling to them as if he would never be able to tear himself free from their embrace. This was great histrionic art. You and I may never attain the heights he scaled, but if we are to climb at all we must pursue a path similar to that which he followed.

The fundamental condition of the art of acting is that everything you do on the stage must have a purpose. This is the first principle you must acquire. It must guide you throughout your study and in all your work on the stage. It is not merely a theoretic principle, but one that must be practised always. It cannot be stressed too much or too often; so let me close this first chapter with the statement that—

EVERYTHING YOU DO ON THE STAGE MUST HAVE A PURPOSE.

SUMMARY

1. In acting there is always the dual problem of interpreting and communicating.

2. Interpretation of character on the stage demands a certain skill. That skill is acting.

3. You must have a purpose all the time you are on the stage.

CHAPTER II

You Must Act all the Time

IT has often been stated that the "art of doing nothing" on the stage is as important and as difficult as anything the actor has to do. Actually it is not possible for an actor to "do nothing" on the stage, and it is of the greatest importance that all who wish to act shall appreciate this undeniable fact. It is not possible to do nothing, and all who are responsible for play production and for training actors should do all in their power to get rid of this phrase, which is harmful. All the time an actor is on the stage he is doing something in view of an audience. The something he is doing should be acting. Everything done on the stage should be contributing something towards the interpretation of the play to the audience.

Perform this little play—

The curtain goes up. Mr. A is standing looking through a note-book. Other characters, Mr. B and Misses C and D, are sitting on the stage. They sit and sit and sit. . . . The curtain comes down.

In this exercise Mr. A is provided with purpose and action. The others are to sit and sit and sit. But you have already observed that all the time you are on the stage you must have a purpose. What purpose have these other three characters? Obviously there cannot be complete freedom for individual imagination, for in this exercise consideration has to be given to the purpose of Mr. A, but, nevertheless, each of these characters must have a purpose in being on the stage, and this imposes upon each the necessity of acting.

If they are to contribute to the interpretation of the play, their interest must be directed towards what Mr. A is doing. If Miss C fidgets with her feet and toys with her dress and glances out towards the audience in search of her friends, or

if Mr. B stares about him or interests himself in one of the
ladies, or if Miss D looks bored because she thinks she has
nothing to do, the attention of the audience will be dis-
tracted from that which should be the focus of interest,
namely, Mr. A, and the members of the audience will become
fidgety because the actors on the stage are fidgety.

For the interpretation of this play—which is not as simple
as it might appear—it is essential for the characters who are
sitting to be completely absorbed in what Mr. A is doing.
They must sit quietly and calmly, and their attention must
not stray for a single moment from Mr. A. They must
endeavour to convey by their attitude towards Mr. A that
they each have an interest in what he is looking for in his
note-book. Mr. A has a definite task, and they also must
have tasks as definite and as important as his.

It cannot be too strongly stressed that all the time you are
on the stage you must have a purpose, and it may perhaps
be useful at times to demand from each actor a statement of
his purpose when he is performing an exercise or a part in
a scene. It is not necessary for the purposes of each of these
characters, Mr. B and Misses C and D, to be exactly
identical. Mr. B might be sceptical of Mr. A's ability to
find what he is looking for. Miss C might be anxious for
him to find it. Miss D might be dreading the result of the
search. Each of the different purposes will impose a difference in the acting of each character, and, if each directs
attention towards the acting of Mr. A, a most interesting
scene will result.

Skill in acting that interprets your own thoughts and at
the same time focuses attention upon another character is
as important as direct acting. It is as important and just as
difficult. Indeed, the task of Mr. A in this exercise is com-
paratively easy, but Miss D will not find it simple to suggest
her dread, nor Miss C her anxiety, nor Mr. B his doubt.
Only after much practice and criticism will the scene be
completely interpreted.

An elaborate variation of this exercise is to be found in

Act I of Bernard Shaw's *Pygmalion*. Under the portico of
Covent Garden are collected a variety of London folk.
Amongst them is the note-taker—Professor Higgins. He is
to be the focus of interest. At first the bystanders take little
or no interest in him, but gradually the action selects him
as the chief personality there, and all the various individuals
become interested in what he is doing. In this scene each of
the characters has a very definite personality to interpret,
yet it is their chief task to focus attention upon Higgins.
For much of the scene they have tasks comparable with the
characters in our exercise. Try this scene yourselves. You
will find it extremely interesting, especially if you concentrate
attention upon the purpose of the scene as well as upon your
own individual task.

A group of ladies would find it interesting and of considerable value to study and rehearse the opening scene of Barrie's
Quality Street. The opening of this scene, you will observe,
is also very similar to the exercise we have just attempted.
Study the opening of the scene down to Miss Susan's
speech—

> Forgive my partiality for romance, Mary. I fear 'tis the
> mark of an old maid.

This is a lovely opening to the play, and establishes the
background of atmosphere against which the play will
develop. It is a prelude which at once introduces the
audience to some of the principal protagonists, and also to
the quaint characteristics of the period and place in which
the action is set.

As the curtain goes up, all the characters are acting—

> *Miss Fanny is reading from a library book while the others
> sew or knit.*

But the knitting and sewing must be contrived to provide
the restful background against which the reading of Miss
Fanny will at once be the focus of interest. It is not until the
audience has had time to appreciate the tendency of the
passage being read that the knitting and sewing, by their

increased speed, really come into the consciousness of the audience. In order to achieve this subordination of the knitting and sewing, it will be necessary for these actresses to go about their tasks in the quietest manner possible, to control their bodies and keep their eyes fixed upon their work.

The increased speed in the knitting and sewing must seem to be the direct result of the thoughts of these ladies as they listen to the passage being read by Miss Fanny. Care must be taken with regard to this apparently simple instruction, or the sudden increase of speed will have the appearance of a stage trick, introduced for the specific purpose of raising a laugh, instead of being the natural result of their reticence with regard to the romantic reference to the male. Their reactions are pointers to their characters, not merely theatrical devices for the amusement of the audience.

Barrie imposes a number of instructions for these ladies throughout this part of the scene, but his instructions are mainly concerned with the physical and outward actions and expressions; the ladies interpreting this scene must also concern themselves with the inward and mental acting that should lead naturally to these outward manifestations. As the curtain rises, the interest in the passage being read is merely general—that polite interest which ladies knitting or sewing give to any conversation at any time. The reading does not disturb their knitting, nor does their knitting disturb the reading. Soon, however, there is a change in the speed at which they work, reflecting the agitation of their thoughts. Each of these individuals will react differently from the others. Miss Willoughby and Miss Susan are the two eldest and they have already resigned themselves to being old maids; but Miss Henrietta has not, nor has Miss Fanny. These two may yet wish "to inspire frenzy in the heart of the male," and, although they have the same reticence with regard to such tales being read aloud, they are still young enough to be thrilled; while even Miss Susan retains sufficient romantic interest to wish to discover how the tale ends. Barrie's instructions are general, but the thoughts of these ladies are individual, and the actresses playing these parts must create the individual thoughts and the physical actions for each separate character in the scene. Miss Henrietta actually does not speak during the part of the scene we are using, but shortly after, when Miss Susan expresses the opinion that she does not expect Miss Phœbe to remain an old maid, she "wistfully" asks—

Do you refer, Miss Susan, to V.B.?

This wistfulness may mark the attitude of Miss Henrietta as she listens to the passage being read by Miss Fanny, and the actress playing this part may wish to suggest this by her silent acting during the reading which causes such a stir in this quiet and peaceful drawing-room.

Rehearse this scene. Concentrate effort upon the silent acting of each of these ladies, so that all contrive to play their parts separately and together for the interpretation of the whole. Rehearse it bit by bit. Firstly, let all the characters be sitting on the stage performing their appropriate tasks of knitting or sewing before the curtain goes up. Miss Fanny is reading. We don't know how long they have been thus employed, but we can assume that it has been for some time, as we know they must shortly be going home. See that there is peace and general restfulness as the curtain goes up, and that the first line is read to indicate that it is a continuation of something that has gone before. The word *Man* breaks the restfulness of the scene. Miss Willoughby will, perhaps, at once work more rapidly; I think Miss Susan may pause and look up before she displays agitation; and it is probable that Miss Henrietta may, even at this point, show something of that wistfulness which marks her general attitude to the subject, and she will display agitation in her work only because the others do.

And rained hot, burning——

They are all eagerly listening now, and this phrase causes Miss Willoughby to exclaim. How will it affect the others?

On eyes, mouth——

Miss Willoughby can stand no more, and she commands
Miss Fanny to stop. But are the others so eager for the book
to be closed?

When the whole of *Quality Street* is being produced with
any but highly skilled actresses, there is insufficient time to
spend long over this delightful opening episode. There is so
much more to be done. Yet, when proper value is given to
the thoughts that move each of these characters, and to their
physical reactions which will communicate them to the
audience, then the joy to both the actors and the audience
is very great indeed. Only by care of this kind to secure
balance between mental and physical acting can you hope
to make characters "live" and give full significance to a
scene. Mental acting provides the soul of character and also
the inner significance of a play.

"Thinking" on the stage and communicating the thoughts
of a character are as difficult as they are important. If you
wish to act, you must cultivate skill in this aspect of the art.
Frequently so much time has to be devoted to the actual
interpretation of the speeches and to other points in production that little time is left for the consideration of mental
acting. Too often it is passed over with some such phrase
as: "You others must take an interest in what is going on."
How they are to achieve this is left to happy chance and to
the glamour of "the night."

A simple, but extremely interesting, play to study is
Saul and David,[1] by Miss Mona Swann. This is a short play
arranged in seven scenes from the Authorized Version of the
Bible. In the third scene of this play we hear Goliath defy and
challenge the people of Israel. We do not see Goliath. He is
"off" stage, and only his voice is heard. On the stage are a
crowd of Israelites and the young boy David.

This scene provides exercise in mental and inward acting
of a most interesting and fascinating kind. The sight of
this giant—as they gaze at him from the stage—wearing
his helmet of brass and his coat of mail, and carrying his great

[1] *Seven Modern Plays* (Nelson).

spear, fills many of the Israelites with fear and despair; while the sound of his voice coming from afar creates an atmosphere of dejection and terror among all the followers of Saul.

Later in this scene Saul and David's brothers watch the boy David gather stones and mount a platform to answer the challenge of Goliath. They hear him speak his defiance to the giant, and they watch him fling the stone that is to kill this mighty champion of the Philistines.

Saul, David's brothers, and those other Israelites who are on the stage during this scene have much to show by their mental acting. Their chief task is to "think" and to communicate "thoughts" to the audience. They have not merely to listen to the speeches of Goliath and David. Each and every one of them has individual thoughts arising from his attitude towards the drama that is going on before his eyes. What are these thoughts that are afflicting each of these warriors as they watch this mere stripling go forth to battle against the mighty giant? Can David, armed with a sling and a few pebbles, destroy the great champion of the dreaded Philistines? What will happen to them all if David fails in his self-sought and impudent task?

It is not sufficient for these actors merely to show an interest in what David and Goliath say and do. They have to find a way of communicating to the audience the thoughts that surge through their minds as they witness the delivery of the Israelites from threatened bondage.

Try some more exercises and concentrate especially upon mental acting—

The curtain goes up. Three people are sitting on the stage listening to a fourth reading a poem. The curtain comes down.

For this exercise let the poem be short, not lasting more than a minute. Concentrate attention on the characters listening to the poem. This exercise should be persisted in until the actors are able to control their limbs, their hands, and their faces, and until they are able to convey to the audience that they are interested in the poem that is being read. It is not sufficient for them to remain still: their faces should express intelligent and understanding interest. On the other hand, they must be made to realize that the audience are supposed to be interested in the poem, not directly in them. The ability to listen without attracting attention to yourself is a most important skill.

In this connexion I recall an incident that took place in a production of *Much Ado About Nothing* many years ago. Claudio was visiting the tomb of the dead Hero. He was accompanied by a number of mourners carrying torches. One of these torch-bearers assumed that he had to display great sorrow. His face was a perfect picture of misery. His expression of extreme dejection caught the attention of the audience; there was at first just a titter from one section, but very soon the whole audience was in an uproar. The scene was ruined. I was Claudio. Perhaps you can imagine my feelings.

Let two ladies play the parts of Viola and Olivia in Shakespeare's *Twelfth Night*. For the purpose of this exercise I suggest a very short passage from Act I, Scene 5—

OLIVIA: . . . Why, what would you?
VIOLA: Make me a willow cabin at your gate,
      And call upon my soul within the house;
      Write loyal cantons of contemned love,
      And sing them loud even in the dead of night;
      Holla your name to the reverberate hills,
      And make the babbling gossip of the air
      Cry out, "Olivia!" O, you should not rest
      Between the elements of air and earth,
      But you should pity me!
OLIVIA: You might do much. What is your parentage?

During the passage spoken by Viola the feelings of Olivia undergo an alarming change towards the pseudo-boy. "His" passionate language stirs up an emotion of love within her, which finds expression in the simple phrase: "You might do much." For Olivia to speak these words with just the right note she must prepare her thoughts during Viola's beautiful speech. Practise this moment of the scene, and concentrate attention upon the acting of Olivia. As the speech gathers intensity and moves towards its climax, the feelings of Olivia come more and more under its influence. Her whole being moves, as it were, towards that of Viola. She comes under the spell of a force too great to be resisted. She must show this to the audience, yet never for one moment may she draw attention away from Viola. The audience should see her only in the margin of consciousness, but should be aware of the effect of Viola's words upon her.

Take passages from any scene you like and treat them in a similar way. At first it may be best to choose passages where only one character speaks. Then the other actor will not be tempted to listen for cues, a habit which does not help towards good acting. Afterwards, choose dialogue passages in which thoughts lead to the right expression for speech.

A magnificent duet which makes a big demand on both characters is that between Bill Crichton and Lady Mary in Act III of *The Admirable Crichton*. From the moment when Crichton begins the speech—

I had nigh forgotten them. He has had his chance, Polly.

to the point when he takes Lady Mary in his arms, the acting of Lady Mary is almost entirely that of the mind. As Crichton talks to her about himself, his achievement, and his vision of himself as a "king," Lady Mary becomes completely fascinated and bewitched. Her entire being radiates her adoration for the majestic figure standing by her side.

At the beginning of this scene Crichton is the central figure; his imposing presence and his fine speech keep him as such. On the other hand, during the earlier part of the scene Lady Mary is but the serving maid of this great man. It is true that she is never servile, but she displays considerable deference towards him, and behaves as an inferior being. When Crichton's conversation becomes more familiar, she drops her menial attitude for a more intimate one. As his purpose becomes clear to her, and realization dawns that he is "making love" to her and actually "proposing" to her, and as his vision is unfolded, the strength of his emotions and his passionate sincerity grip her whole being, and the tenseness of her emotions becomes as great as his. She contributes but a few brief phrases in this important duet, but the transition of her thoughts, the strength of her emotion, and the expression of her love must be interpreted by the power of her mental acting.

At the same time it should be realized that the significance and the poetic vision of Crichton's fine romantic language may be communicated only through the force and passion arising from his thoughts. Direct and mental acting are demanded from both Crichton and Lady Mary throughout this great romantic scene. Success in the interpretation of this scene will depend very much upon the intensity of the thoughts and feelings of the two protagonists.

You must act all the time you are on the stage. First you must determine the purpose for which you are there, then you must find a way of fulfilling this purpose and of communicating it to the audience. It is not enough merely to behave while on the stage. This usually is little short of misbehaviour and brings about some unfortunate effect. Your acting must be definite and purposeful.

SUMMARY

1. You must act all the time you are on the stage.

2. It is not possible to "do nothing" on the stage.

3. An actor should be able to state his purpose for being on the stage.

4. "Thinking" on the stage and communicating the thoughts of a character are as difficult as they are important.

5. **Ability to listen without attracting attention to yourself is a most important skill.**
6. **It is not enough merely to behave while on the stage.**
7. **Acting must be definite and purposeful.**

EXERCISES ON CHAPTER II

1. *The Merchant of Venice:* Act IV, Scene 1.
Play the part of Shylock during Portia's speech—
> The quality of mercy is not strained.

2. *Twelfth Night:* Act III, Scene 4.
Play the part of Viola during Antonio's two speeches—
> Let me speak a little. This youth that you see here.

and
> But O! how vile an idol proves this god!

3. *A Midsummer Night's Dream:* Act IV, Scene 1.
Play the part of Bottom waking from his enforced sleep.

4. *Julius Caesar.*
Study any of the crowd scenes. Note the reactions of the crowd to the speeches of Marullus and Brutus, and especially to the oration of Mark Antony.

5. *Julius Caesar:* Act IV, Scene 3.
Study this scene and note particularly the effect of the words of Brutus upon the mind of Cassius.

6. *Hamlet:* Act I, Scene 2.
Play Hamlet during the opening speeches of this scene. (Read the description of John Gielgud during this scene given in *John Gielgud's Hamlet,* by Rosamond Gilder.)

7. *King Lear:* Act I, Scene 1.
Play the part of Cordelia during the protestations of love by her sisters.

8. *Will Shakespeare,* by Clemence Dane: Act III, Scene 1.
Play the part of Will Shakespeare during Henslowe's description of how he saw Anne at Stratford, beginning—
> Yet I did see her.
> Making for London, not a week ago.

Search for the thoughts that Henslowe's words call up into the mind of Shakespeare.

9. *Will Shakespeare:* Act II, Scene 1.
Play the part of Mary during Shakespeare's speech—
    You should not laugh. I tell you such a thought.

10. *Children in Uniform,* by Christa Winsloe: Act III, Scene 3.
Play the part of Manuela during Fraulein von Bernburg's speech—
    No, Manuela, a friend. Don't upset yourself so.

11. *My Lady's Dress,* by Edward Knoblock: Act II, Scene 1.
Rehearse the duologue between Jonkheer and Antje, paying particular attention to the mental acting of Antje.

12. *The Lady with a Lamp,* by Reginald Berkeley: Act I, Scene 2.
The dialogue between Florence Nightingale and Henry Tremayne is particularly interesting as being the result of intense thought and feeling. While the speeches of Florence are always in response to those of Tremayne, they are far more arguments from her own chain of thoughts on the subject under discussion. Rehearse this scene and pay attention to the inner thoughts of each of the protagonists.

13. *The Barretts of Wimpole Street,* by Rudolf Besier: Act IV.
Rehearse the duologue between Robert Browning and Elizabeth Barrett from the entrance of Browning to his exit. Search for the mental reactions of Elizabeth.

14. *The Confidential Clerk,* by T. S. Eliot: Act II.
Rehearse the dialogue between Colby Simpkins and Lucasta Angel in The Flat in the Mews. A study in revelations and their effects.

15. *Reunion,* by W. St. John Tayleur.
The entrance of "The Figure" in this one-act play presents interesting problems for each of the players already on the stage. Their reactions to this entering figure will reveal something of their individual characters, thoughts, and degree of excitement and pleasure.

16. *Where the Cross is Made,* by Eugene O'Neill.
Rehearse the part of Doctor Higgins in the opening dialogue between him and Nat Bartlett and try to reveal the Doctor's reactions to the amazing story unfolded by Nat.

CHAPTER III

THE ACTOR'S MEDIUM

A PLAY is something that is both seen and heard. The visual accompaniments of vocalization are essential parts of acting. Indeed, what an actor does is frequently as effective as what he says. Long after the spoken word is forgotten, a vivid picture of some movement, posture, or gesture may be retained in the memory.

The body may be a potent force in revealing character. The motionless pose of John Gielgud in the second scene of *Hamlet* achieved a powerful expression of scorn, unwilling obedience, and pent up emotions. Words could not have revealed greater bitterness or distaste than did this silent, immobile figure. John Gielgud possesses a wonderful acting instrument, each part of which is flexible and beautiful. Throughout his performance of Hamlet we saw him using and controlling every part of this instrument. Pose, movement, gesture were all combined with sensitive and clear vocalization to reveal, in the person of this great actor, the character and personality of Prince Hamlet.

Drama is concerned with showing characters and their conflicts—not merely telling something about them. It does not describe characters, but presents them to us. The actor has to create the illusion of being the character. To the audience he must *be* Hamlet, Shylock, Micawber, or Uriah Heep. In a novel we read about the lives of characters; in a play we see them living. We hear them speak, laugh, and weep; we also see them moving and behaving.

The physical qualities are often as distinctive as are the mental qualities. Many characters, both in real life and in drama, owe their existence in the minds of others to their physical characteristics. Sir Herbert Tree appreciated this fact, and used it as the foundation of his work on the stage. To him physical attributes were of the greatest importance.

His critics abused him for his over-elaboration of details of
gesture and physical qualities, and for his almost complete
disregard of the finer mental qualities of character. His
critics were probably right. But it is nevertheless true that,
with regard to many of the characters interpreted by Tree,
his attitude was absolutely justifiable. His study of Svengali
was built up on an elaborate and unforgettable system of
gesture.

The supreme example of character creation by means of
gesture is, of course, Charlie Chaplin, whose movement,
posture, and gesture develop into an elaborate, rhythmical
creation. His acting becomes a deeply symbolical dance
every detail of which is significant and revealing. Words
would add nothing to our knowledge of the characters he
has portrayed, nothing to their emotions or their thoughts.
For him the body—especially the feet, hands, and face—is
the entire instrument. The voice is unnecessary.

Sir Andrew Aguecheek in *Twelfth Night* regrets that he
has not spent "the time in the tongues" that he has "in
fencing and dancing." Here is the clue that helps us to
understand this character, and the actor must carry the
implication of these words with him throughout his interpretation. This elegant figure of a man actually dances his
way through this delightful comedy. The exquisite and
delicate humour of Andrew lies much in his graceful antics
and gestures. Similarly with Mr. Coade in Barrie's *Dear
Brutus*. The actor playing these characters is called upon to
work out and develop movement and gesture which, by
their rhythm and accent, will convey to an audience the
real significance of these charming, inconsequent beings.
There can be little wonder that perhaps the greatest interpreter of these two characters was the same man—the late
Mr. Norman Forbes.

It is of importance, however, that we should remind ourselves that a dramatist expresses himself through the medium
of language. One of the chief purposes of acting and
dramatic presentation is to make clear the meaning of the

author's words. By sympathetic vocalization an actor may interpret to his audience the deepest refinements of thought and feeling. The power of vocal expression cannot be too greatly emphasized. It is at once the first and the finest achievement in the art of the theatre. By the right use of voice the actor not only enters into a sympathetic understanding of the character he is interpreting, but at the same time he enables his audience to appreciate his intentions and compels them to accept the illusion for reality.

The permanent and essential vehicles of dramatic expression are speech, movement, and gesture. These must be the means by which the actor interprets and communicates the intentions of the dramatist to an audience. His instrument is his whole body: his voice, his face, his hands, his feet. By the control and co-ordination of these he will perform his task, which is to reveal character and the significance of the spoken word.

There is some justification for thinking that all too many of those taking part in the performances of plays have given very little thought to the instrument they are using for their interpretations. Even professional actors are sometimes inaudible, and often the desire to appear natural has divorced acting almost entirely from the stage. The movement towards realism and naturalism on the stage was inevitable. It was a logical revolt against artificiality and gross exaggeration. Among other things, it opposed the strident movement, the obtrusive gesture, and the declamatory speech found in the decadent theatre of the late Victorian era. It did not, however, deny the need for controlled movement, appropriate gesture, and audible speech; nor did it postulate anything contrary to the fundamental purpose of acting, which is to communicate a recorded story to an audience.

There is a common belief that interpretation and communication will follow naturally upon understanding and feeling. Actors are invited to understand the meaning of the language they are to speak, and to suffer the emotions of the characters they are to interpret, with the devout assurance that they will then be able to express these to an audience. This is very similar to saying that, if I understand and appreciate the musical meaning and significance of a Chopin Nocturne, I shall be able to interpret it upon a pianoforte; or that, because I am sensitive to colour and natural formations, I shall be able to paint on a canvas my impressions of a landscape. Nothing could be wider of the mark. In addition to understanding the values and significance of language, and, perhaps, feeling the emotions of the character, the actor must possess a voice, body, and face sufficiently flexible to express a vast range of ideas and emotions, and he must have the skill to control all these parts so that they will do his bidding at any given time.

SUMMARY

1. **The visual accompaniments of vocalization are essential parts of acting.**

2. **The body may be a potent force in revealing character.**

3. **Drama is concerned with** *showing* **characters and their conflicts.**

4. **Physical qualities are often as distinctive as mental qualities.**

5. **The power of vocal expression cannot be too greatly emphasized.**

6. **The permanent and essential vehicles of dramatic expression are speech, movement, and gesture.**

7. **The actor's instrument is his whole body—his voice, his face, his hands, his feet—and these must be both flexible and under control.**

CHAPTER IV

THE VOICE

THAT audibility is the first duty of the actor seems to be such an obvious fact that it should not need emphasis. Yet, even in the professional theatre of to-day, actors are frequently at fault in thinking that natural speech is of greater importance than audibility. The desire to be natural and intimate on the stage, and an absurd belief that the curtain represents the "fourth wall" of a room, lead many actors to ignore the audience. In doing so they fail to communicate their story or their character to those on the other side of the footlights. It is not possible to be natural on the stage. And because communication is a condition of acting, and the space in which the actor has to achieve this is large, it follows that everything done on the stage must be on a larger and broader scale than in ordinary life, and that speech must be of a specialized kind to fulfil the conditions *natural* to the theatre and the drama.

At times actors are so much concerned with the interpretation of character that they forget the necessity of making themselves audible. In one scene of *Much Ado About Nothing* Borachio is drunk. But in this very scene Shakespeare makes him confess to his friend Conrade the part he has played in the plot against Claudio. This confession is apparently the idle boasting of one in his cups, but actually it is the means used by Shakespeare to communicate important information to the audience. The actor must preserve the illusion of being very, very drunk, but at the same time he must see that the audience does not miss a single word. Failure to achieve this will mean that the audience will lack certain knowledge of what has taken place, and will in consequence not be able to follow intelligently the subsequent development of the drama.

It is of importance that the speech of an actor should seem

to be the natural speech of the character, and it is undoubtedly proper for him to interpret his character, but in doing so he must at the same time be distinct and audible. This, as I have said, is the actor's first duty.

In order to achieve audibility it is not necessary to shout, nor indeed is it always necessary to speak loudly. A whisper is audible if it is produced properly. To secure audibility, strong and flexible lips are essential, and consonants must be clearly and firmly articulated. All who wish to speak in public should study voice production in order to secure proper breath control and a good resonant voice. Practise humming and exercises with words beginning with the *m* sound. Stress the consonant and lengthen it before passing to the vowel. Don't be afraid of sound. You will not make too much noise. Many folk think they are shouting when actually the sounds coming from their mouths would not disturb a mouse.

The plays of Shakespeare provide many exercises which will help you to concentrate on being audible. Choose some of the dramatic and declamatory speeches from such a play as *Julius Caesar*. In your practice exaggerate the importance of the consonants. Articulate them firmly and incisively. Study the speech of Marullus in the first scene, beginning—

Wherefore rejoice? What conquest brings he home?

This is a splendid dramatic and vigorous speech which can hardly be spoken too loudly. Let yourself go. Let the crowd have the full force of your bitter anger and sarcasm. Concentrate attention upon the consonants and I think you will readily discern that, in addition to their importance with regard to audibility, they are also of considerable dramatic value. Notice the dramatic effect of the recurring *s* sound.

Speak the speech again and again. You will soon feel the urge to greater intensity and greater speed. Choose other speeches for yourself. You will find many, both in the plays of Shakespeare and in modern plays, which will provide you with a similar opportunity to employ the full volume of your voice.

Actors are sometimes advised to speak slowly in order that they may be heard. This is not good advice. It is very similar to saying that a march should be played slowly in order that the members of a band may play the notes correctly. Once I had the misfortune to march behind such a band. We soldiers told that band what it should do. I tell you the same. Go home and learn how to speak both slowly and quickly. Of course, gabbling is never permissible, but that must not be confused with a fast delivery. Gabbling is a careless and uncontrolled form of speech which must be cured by cultivating the practice of differentiating the words in a phrase or sentence. Its cure involves paying attention to articulation, not to speed of delivery. It will be cured by insistence upon the values of consonants, by the phrasing of speeches, and by marking breathing places as the singer does in his songs.

Speed is not related to audibility. SPEED DEPENDS UPON CHARACTER AND UPON THE PURPOSE OF THE LANGUAGE SPOKEN.

The character of Fluellen in *Henry V* demands rapid speech. His irascibility and quick temper, his impatience and intolerance, combined with his conceit and self-assurance, are best interpreted by facile thought and rapid vocalization. It is not possible, I think, to speak his lines too quickly. At the same time, the actor must, by intonation and inflexion, indicate that he is a Welshman, and he must be audible. Anything but quick delivery is contradictory to the character of Fluellen. His mind is ever alert, he is quick to take offence, and exceptionally quick-witted. All his actions are as sharp and rapid as his thought, and his speech accompanies his movement and his passionate patriotism.

Similarly with Professor Higgins in *Pygmalion*. This excitable, enthusiastic, and eager professor of phonetics speaks with a rapidity to match his alert brain. He sweeps all obstacles from his path by the torrent of language that he always has at his command. For those who desire an excellent exercise for controlled rapid speech, I strongly recommend the exciting duet at the close of Act III of this play. Here Professor Higgins and Colonel Pickering tell Mrs. Higgins how they work with and care for Eliza. Gradually their enthusiasm carries them away, and, in their great excitement, both talk together, getting ever more heated, until they are finally stopped by Mrs. Higgins. Here is a really fine exercise in rapid speaking that must be controlled. These two men must speak this duet with the same regard to time and pace that singers of musical duets have to observe.

Actually speed is just as important in speech as it is in music. In drama the time and the speed signatures must be sought for in the character and in the language. Take down your copy of Barrie's *The Admirable Crichton* again and compare the character of Lady Mary Lasenby in Act I with the same girl in Act III. In Act I she is indolent and lazy. Her movements are slow, and her speech, when she finds sufficient energy for this tiring task, is leisurely and languorous. But on the island, under the dictatorship rule of the erstwhile butler, she is a new being. She is "tingling with vitality," her movement is swift and her speech is vivacious. Read her description of how she hunted and caught a buck in Firefly Grove. Here is a narrative of a hunt, but it is something more than this. Its true significance emphasizes the effect that life on the island has had upon Mary Lasenby. It implies something of the glamour of the island life, and expresses the elation Mary feels in her new-found freedom and her joy in living. This emotion demands considerable vivacity for its interpretation. Diction must be lively to be in sympathy with the mood of the speaker. She is eager to tell the tale of her adventure which ended in such glorious success, but in the telling she catches again the spirit of the chase, and her speech increases in speed until it moves with the rapidity of the chase itself.

On the other hand, it is sometimes necessary to speak slowly and with deliberation. Not all characters demand rapid speech, and language often calls for slow delivery in its true interpretation.

Read over the first scene of *The Merchant of Venice* and try to *feel* the changes in speed of the various speeches of Antonio, Salanio, and Salarino. Antonio opens the scene quietly and sadly. His speech is moderately slow. All Salarino's speeches, on the other hand, contain imagery that expresses lively movement, vigorous, and even turbulent. The general movement of his language would seem to be fast, and sometimes it moves with great speed. The language of Salanio, however, while not sad or solemn, lacks the vigour of that of Salarino. Read these opening speeches and give them their appropriate speeds. When you have felt and expressed the difference between the speeds of the various speeches, try to discover the variety of speed within each separate speech. For, while there is a general time for each speech, there are also considerable variety and change of speed within the speeches themselves.

Turn to Act II, Scene 8, of this play, and again study the speeches of Salarino and Salanio. You will readily observe that Shakespeare has preserved the relative speeds for the language of these two characters. Speed is a quality of character and language; it is an essential part of dramatic dialogue, which imposes a condition of speech upon the actor.

The ear of the actor must be trained to be sensitive to pace, rhythm, and tone. These are as intentional in drama as they are in music. VARIETY FOR ITS OWN SAKE IS AS IRRITATING AS THE LACK OF IT IS MONO-TONOUS. There should be variety, but it should be purposeful. Variety in speed is derived from character and language, and not from the actor's desire for it. Design in pace and stress provides rhythm in speech; variety without design is purposeless, distracting, and confusing.

Take up any play. Study various speeches, and try to develop sensitiveness to the pace at which they should be spoken. Whenever you read a play, try to feel the changes of "time" as they are affected by the language spoken and by the characters themselves.

At the same time you must endeavour to acquire facility in speaking rapidly. To do so you must persist in cultivating strong lips, you must articulate consonants with the utmost care and precision, and you must exercise the tongue to increase its flexibility. It is also necessary to acquire at the same time control over the organs of speech, so that you can speak quickly or slowly as required by the text.

Always there is this dual task before the actor—the task of selecting and that of performing. They are separate and distinct. The actor must prepare for both. He must acquire the skill to perform and he must cultivate the sensitiveness to select. By practice he can acquire the skill, and, by assiduous care in listening to others, by honest self-criticism, and by experience in life he can develop the power to select.

Speaking generally, the language of romance moves with speed. Its purpose is to stimulate emotional sympathy and excitement, and to create an atmosphere of lyrical beauty and glamour. The love scenes between Paolo and Francesca must concentrate attention upon the aesthetic beauty of love, and never allow the mind to dwell upon the ethical or social aspects of such an illicit liaison. The world of romance is an irrational one. It must make its appeal to the senses, not to reason. Speed alone can achieve that "ready suspension of disbelief" which is a condition of all art.

Compare the language of Bassanio with that of Shylock. Bassanio's appeal is to the emotions, that of Shylock is to reason. Shylock would have you think logically; he is eager to convince his hearers of the reasonableness of his actions and his demands. Argument makes its appeal to the mind. It develops slowly, because it must encourage thought. But, while the general *tempo* of Bassanio's language is considerably faster than that of Shylock, there will be found far greater variety of speed in the language of Shylock than in that of Bassanio.

Similarly, if we compare the language of Brutus with that of Cassius, we find that the variety of speed in the language of

Brutus is considerably greater than in that of Cassius. The actions of Brutus are controlled by the cold logic of the mind, those of Cassius by a passionate sense of civic justice. The language of Cassius is born of his feelings of discontent with the turn of political power. The language of Brutus is the expression of convictions arrived at after careful thought and reasoning. The mind of Brutus embraces a vaster range of thought than does that of Cassius; its scope is wider, and its variety greater. The speed at which the language is to be spoken must be determined by considerations of character and language, and by the effect that you desire to make on your audience.

Tone in speech is, perhaps, of even greater importance than speed. It is elusive, but when the right tone is found its effectiveness is far greater than any visual effect can possibly be. Tonal quality of voice can be acquired by the study and practice of voice production, by correct breathing, and by the true enunciation of vowel sounds.

During the past decade the general standard of speech has improved considerably. Educational bodies have stressed its value, and to-day some study of speech is regarded as essential. In many schools, elementary, secondary, and private, the spoken language is considered to be of prime importance, while in some (notably in secondary and private schools for girls) the study of verse speaking has developed not only a high standard of speech, but also a hitherto un-known sensibility to language. The tonal quality of the voices of young women to-day is, generally speaking, very fine indeed. It is a delight to hear them speak. They are almost as careful and proud of their voices as they are of their hair. Would that I could say the same of the young men! Perhaps we can find consolation in the thought that, where the young women go to-day, the young men will follow to-morrow.

But tonal quality alone is not sufficient. Frequently we find ourselves too consciously aware of a beautiful voice. This is often due to the fact that, while the tones are of themselves beautiful, they are unrelated to the content of the language spoken. GOOD SPEECH WILL DIRECT ATTENTION TO THAT WHICH IS SPOKEN, NOT TO THE INSTRUMENT OF VOICE.

Intimately connected with tone are the questions of range and control of pitch. It has been estimated that a compass of at least two octaves is necessary. However this may be, the power of control is absolutely essential to all who may wish to speak in public. The control of pitch and the selection of tune are of the greatest importance for all who would attain success in the interpretation of the drama. Tune, or sequence of tones, is the most potent force in speech. It affects both the meaning of a sentence and its emotional implication.

Apply tunes to the following question—

"*Mary, where are you?*"

(*a*) You are calling your little girl: "Mary, where are you?"

(*b*) You call: "Mary, where are you?" There is no answer. You call again: "Mary, where are you?" Again there is no answer. You call again and again.

(*c*) A young lover calls: "Mary, where are you?"

(*d*) Mary has suddenly disappeared. Anxiously you search and call out again and again: "Mary, where are you?"

The tunes are infinite. They will embrace a variety of tones, of pace, of emphasis. Some tunes will demand short or even staccato vowel sounds, while others will require them to be lengthened considerably. Always in these exercises the words are the same. But their implications and emotional stresses vary, and these variations will be expressed by the tunes in which they are spoken.

Turn to the last act of *The Merchant of Venice*. Speak Lorenzo's speech—

> How sweet the moonlight sleeps upon this bank !
> Here will we sit, and let the sounds of music
> Creep in our ears: soft stillness and the night

> Become the touches of sweet harmony.
> Sit, Jessica. Look, how the floor of heaven
> Is thick inlaid with patines of bright gold:
> There's not the smallest orb which thou behold'st
> But in his motion like an angel sings,
> Still quiring to the young-eyed cherubims,—
> Such harmony is in immortal souls;
> But whilst this muddy vesture of decay
> Doth grossly close it in, we cannot hear it.

This is a beautiful speech to practise for the cultivation of tone, for correct vowel sounds, and for studying tune. For Lorenzo the world is full of song and sweet music. His mind is far removed from the discordant and harsh realities of this world; he is dwelling in a serene and spiritual world of his own, created from the tenderness of his passion for Jessica. There is a fine ecstasy of calm serenity and perfect peace. Perhaps the key of the tune is in the two words, "Sit, Jessica." In ten years' time these two words may not be spoken with the same tender implication. Once you have found the right tune for these two words, you will have discovered the key in which the whole speech has to be delivered.

Study Act I, Scene 5, of *Twelfth Night* again, especially the dialogue between Olivia and Viola. Follow the changing moods of these two protagonists. Notice that Olivia suddenly changes from prose to verse. Why? Has Shakespeare a purpose in this, or is it just accidental? What has happened to Olivia? The style of her language changes; so must the manner of her speech. The tune of her speech must reveal the secret of her heart.

A wonderful scene, this, for the study of tone values. Make a special study of Viola's speech beginning—

> Make me a willow cabin at your gate

This speech indicates clearly, I think, that the effectiveness of speech is due to a sequence of tones and their relation to one another. Continuity of speech, thought, and character depends upon the fitness of the sequence of tones and the intervals of pitch. This is as true of speech as it is of music. Monotone has its own peculiar effect, and so have every modulation and sequence of pitch. Speak this speech with gradually rising pitch towards "Cry out Olivia." Then come down in pitch and with some intensity speak the last lines—

> . . . O, you should not rest
> Between the elements of air and earth,
> But you should pity me !

This is the climax of the speech. Frequently it becomes only an anticlimax. These lines must be spoken in tones contrasting with, yet directly resulting from, those that have preceded them. There is a contrast in pitch, but the notes must be in harmony with those already used. It is not possible to indicate exactly the tune for this or any other speech. Each speaker must compose his own tune. Choice of tune is an essential task of the actor, and by his choice he conveys his intimacy with the emotional stress of the character he is portraying. If his tones and tune are entirely in sympathy with the character and the emotions implied by the language, he will create a sincere illusion of "living the part."

Turn to that charming speech of Lob to his flowers in Act I of *Dear Brutus*. Suit your tones to the implication of language and to the character of Lob. Remember his extreme age, his passionate love of flowers, his sincere belief in their sensitiveness and understanding. Try to feel his changing moods as he speaks to each separate bloom: his tender affection, his playfulness, the pain he suffers over their troubles, and his elation over the beauty of their perfume.

SINCERITY DEPENDS UPON THE FITNESS OF TUNE AND GESTURE.

It is not possible to give rules for finding tunes; to say that this tune will fit this situation or that another tone will be an apt expression for that mood. Perhaps it is just as well.

The joy is in the search. But do not let the absence of any
hard and fast rules be an excuse for tones being haphazard
and things of fancy. Tones and tune, like everything else,
must have their definite purpose.

Audiences are very responsive to tones. By right tones an
actor may move an audience to the highest pitch of excitement and feeling; he may control thought and win the
deepest sympathy. On the other hand, tones may arouse
resentment, opposition, and antipathy. The sudden introduction of an unsuspected tone may even turn the most
serious moments into ones of merriment. This is at once a
warning to the tragedian and romantic actor, and a service
to the comedian.

A great comedian is usually a master of tones. He knows
that appropriate tone conveys the true intent of what he has
to say. Relative humour depends almost entirely upon tone
for its interpretation. "It is not so much what he says, as
how he says it."

Professor Higgins is a master of phonetics. He is a master
of vowel sounds. He is also a student and master of tone and
tune. In his interpretation of this character it is important
for the actor to reveal this fact. In Act II of *Pygmalion* he has
abundant opportunity. With tones he plays upon Eliza,
Mrs. Pearce, and Doolittle in turn. Read this act again, and
try to *hear* the variety of tones underlying the speeches of
Higgins. Inwardly he was never more serious in his life. A
great "folly" inspires his thought. He realizes the opportunity of establishing the truth of his conviction that he can
create a new being from this "draggletailed guttersnipe."
His extravagant and bombastic language serves as an escape
mechanism from the thoughts that are aroused by the task
before him and the possibility of its achievement. The
language he uses, especially in his speeches to Eliza, serves
more as a cloak to hide his real thoughts than as a medium
for revealing them. To all but Colonel Pickering, who is
also a student of phonetics and is interested as a fellow
scientist, Higgins appears to be mad, stupid, or flippant. To

Eliza he is just "barmy," because she can understand only the literal significance of his language; to Doolittle he is just another of those men of the world out for a good time at the expense of women; to Mrs. Pearce, who understands something of his cleverness, he is obstinate and foolish. The task of the actor is a difficult one. The tones must reveal the complexity of his mood. Except for brief moments, the tones will be remote from the literal meaning—they will be unsuspected ones, to suggest the implications of the language and the humour of this great "reformer."

One of the most important aspects of speech, and one that is most neglected, is that of *stress*. By stress, or emphasis, a speaker directs attention to what is most important in what he has to say. The words of a sentence are not of equal value, nor are the phrases and sentences in a speech. It is the speaker's business to decide the relative importance of words, phrases, and sentences, and to take steps to make these clear to his audience. The meaning and implication of a sentence may be entirely changed by the application of emphasis to different words.

Lecturers sometimes complain that their students have completely misunderstood the purport of their lecture. Nine times out of ten the fault is with the lecturer. He has taken no pains in the preparation of the delivery of his lecture. To very many lecturers the method of delivery is a matter of no concern at all. They just drawl out their sentences one after the other, with a complete disregard of articulation, tone, or stress. False emphasis is too common amongst lecturers, preachers, and actors. It indicates either that the speaker does not understand the significance of language himself, or that he is utterly indifferent to the real purpose of speech.

By right emphasis the speaker directs attention to the purpose of the language. It is the vital part of speech, providing shape and form to the language spoken, and moulding and controlling the impressions of those who listen.

The vocalization of modern dramatic dialogue demands the closest attention to stress and phrasing.

Take down your copy of Galsworthy's *Loyalties*, and turn to Gilman's speech in Act III, Scene 1, beginning—

Well, I've come to you from a sense of duty, sir, and also from a feelin' of embarrassment.

Personality and character are indicated by the irrelevance of much that Gilman says, as well as by the hint of a Cockney dialect. But the personality of Gilman is really only of secondary importance. The main purpose of this speech lies in the narrative of evidence which establishes Dancy's guilt.

By correct phrasing and the stressing of important words, emphasis must be given to those parts of the speech which are directly concerned with this evidence. In your copy differentiate the direct narrative from the irrelevancies; phrase the speech to indicate Gilman's trend of thought, and underline words and phrases of importance. Now speak the speech, and try to emphasize its purpose and at the same time to indicate Gilman's personality.

Simple, direct prose is a feature of modern drama. It gives dramatic dialogue a strong resemblance to the language of everyday life. This use of the current vernacular has led to an erroneous belief that contemporary dramatic dialogue is easier to speak than that of the older dramatists. Turn to Act III, Scene 3, of *Loyalties*—the dialogue between Mabel and Dancy. Rarely in this scene does emotion get the upper hand, yet we are always aware of the tense feelings of the protagonists. The atmosphere is grim, while each character speaks simple and direct sentences and phrases. Any one will be able to speak the language, but great skill will be required for the interpretation of the psychological implications and tense emotions that lie suppressed.

Compare the language of *Loyalties* with that of *The Merchant of Venice*. Take the two speeches of De Levis towards the end of Act III, Scene 2, and compare them with any two speeches of Shylock. Compare them with Shylock's speech to the Duke in Act IV, Scene 1—

I have possess'd your Grace of what I purpose.

Can it be said that it is simpler to give a full interpretation of the significance of the words spoken by De Nevis than of those addressed to the Duke by Shylock? I do not think so.

To gain skill in the interpretation of modern dialogue it is of the greatest importance that you should practise reading aloud until you have cultivated a sense of the dramatic values of stress, phrasing, and pausing. Turn to Act III, Scene 2, of *Loyalties*, and study the dialogue between Twisden and Dancy. Search the dialogue for its specific dramatic purpose, for the personalities of the two characters. Phrase the speeches, and underline and stress words which emphasize the dramatic significance of the dialogue. Always remember that it is the mental conflict that is of importance. Ask yourself, "What are the thoughts of these characters during the dialogue?"

Stress not only gives emphasis to the significance and meaning of language; it indicates the strength of emotional feeling. No one who saw *Mourning Becomes Electra*, by Eugene O'Neill, will ever forget the terrific stress Miss Laura Cowie gave to—

Leave me alone! Stop nagging at me with your crazy suspicions!

as she began to snap under the strain of listening to the accusing suggestions of her husband. Nor will they ever forget the terrifying emphasis that Robert Harris gave to—

I murdered her!

towards the end of Act V of the second part of this great trilogy.

Throughout this play intensity of speech and movement must be used to give emphasis to the terrible mental conflicts suffered by the chief characters. Stress, phrasing, and pauses must be studied and applied to give rhythm to the swift movement of the drama, and to convey the sense of impending fate and inevitable retribution. In such a play it is as important to select moments for stressing emotion as it is to select moments for stressing the meaning of language.

Phrases, sentences, and indeed whole speeches have to be stressed beyond all others in order that overwhelming passion, fear, hatred, or love may be emphasized and made to stand out in proper relationship to the rest of the play.

Naturalist dialogue may be tantalizingly difficult to speak. Get a copy of Merton Hodge's *The Wind and the Rain*, and turn to Act II, Scene 2—the dialogue between Charles and Anne. Look at the short sentences: some of them are not more than two or three words. Does the language in this scene convey personality and character? What is the dramatic purpose of this scene? Note the quietness of the scene, and especially note the intense quietness of its climax. Its silence is emphatic.

Read this scene aloud and try to visualize these two young people as they sit together in that small lodging. Hear in your mind the quiet conversation, with its delicate insinuation and its psychological implications. The close intimacy of the dialogue and of the characters is apt to cause the actors to forget their prime purpose, which is to communicate the play to the audience. The desire to express faithfully the intimate and natural attitude of Charles and Anne tends towards underacting and speech that conveys little or nothing of its purpose to those on the other side of the footlights.

Detailed intimacy of family life is displayed in Miss Dodie Smith's *Call it a Day*. Dialogue is most carefully selected to give a natural resemblance to that of everyday life in the modern family circle. Audibility is essential if the humour of this delightful play is to be appreciated by an audience, and the great variety of character and personality may be interpreted only by studied and appropriate use of speed, tone, pitch, stress, and pause.

The voice must always be the chief medium of expression in the theatre. In recent years there has been a tendency in the professional theatre to extend the importance of lighting and *décor*. These are of considerable value in assisting the actor, and are of great interest to the audience; but, so long as the drama is concerned with human conflicts and emotions, it must be interpreted mainly by speech. In the past it was the carpenter and painter, now it would seem to be the electrician who would usurp the supreme position in the theatre. But this must not, cannot, be. Drama is a human, not a mechanical, document. No matter how symbolic or naturalistic or rational visual effects may be, they can never attain the same power over thought and emotion as the human voice.

SUMMARY

1. To be audible is the first duty of an actor.

2. Speech must be of a specialized kind to fulfil the conditions natural to the theatre and the drama.

3. Speed in speech depends upon character and the purpose of the language spoken.

4. In drama the time and speed signatures must be sought for in the character and in the language.

5. Pace, rhythm, and tone are as intentional in drama as they are in music.

6. Variety for its own sake is as irritating as the lack of it is monotonous.

7. Speaking generally, the language of romance moves with speed.

8. Good speech will direct attention to that which is spoken, not to the instrument of voice.

9. Sincerity depends upon the fitness of tune and gesture.

10. By right emphasis the speaker directs attention to the purpose of the language.

EXERCISES ON CHAPTER IV

1. *The Merchant of Venice:* Act IV, Scene 1. Shylock's speech—
    I have possess'd your Grace of what I purpose.
Note the emphatic beginning and the measured threat, followed by a pause for its effect upon those present in the Court. The argument that

follows is not weighty, but scornful and almost flippant. It gathers speed. Then another pause in preparation for—

Now, for your answer.

In the last few lines may be found considerable variety of speed. At first the language gathers speed, which is checked by the line—

So can I give no reason, nor I will not.

The rest is measured and bitter.

2. Shylock's speech in the same scene—

What judgment shall I dread, doing no wrong?

Again, as you read this speech note the great variety of speed as phrases illustrating Shylock's thoughts follow each other with considerable rapidity. Again the speech begins in measured and assured manner, but Shylock's facility in the use of argument to press home his thoughts compels speech to move in sympathy with the pace of his mental images.

3. In this same scene compare the two speeches of Antonio—

I pray you think, you question with the Jew

and

But little: I am armed and well prepared.

Note how these speeches move easily, almost without interruption. There would seem to be little variety in emotion, little that is stressed beyond the rest; all is smooth and even and tranquil. Quiet resignation and a placid acceptance of an inevitable fate mark all that Antonio has to say.

4. *The Merchant of Venice:* Act III, Scene 2. Bassanio's speech—

So may the outward shows be least themselves:

It should be noted that this speech actually follows Bassanio's decision to choose the leaden casket. He has examined the caskets while Portia has been speaking; he has made his choice while the song has been sung. This speech presents an emotional outburst. It moves forward with considerable speed towards the moment when he exclaims—

Thy paleness moves me more than eloquence;
And here choose I—joy be the consequence!

Compare this speech with those of Shylock already given. Note the difference of speed required, and especially the greater variety of speed needed for the interpretation of Shylock's speeches.

5. *Julius Caesar:* Act II, Scene 3. Calpurnia's speech—

Caesar, I have never stood on ceremonies,
Yet now they fright me.

Phrase and emphasize important words to indicate clearly its meaning and the superstitious fear. Note the climax.

6. *The Lady with a Lamp*, by Reginald Berkeley: Act I, Scene 1.
Study this scene and try to get the time signature for the various

characters. Note the terse and incisive comments and questions of Mrs. Nightingale, the heavily-weighted statements of Lord Palmerston, the petulance of William Nightingale, the rather shallow dialogue of Elizabeth Herbert, and the lively enthusiasm of Florence Nightingale, her sincerity and depth of thought.

Compare these various characters and their language, and note how speed is affected.

7. *The Lady with a Lamp:* Act I, Scene 2. Florence Nightingale's speech to the fountain beginning—

Fountain! Why are we given conflicting natures?

Study this speech carefully. Soliloquy is rare in modern drama. What is the purpose of this soliloquy? Note the variety of pace to correspond with the conflicting thoughts. Phrase the speech, underline outstanding words and phrases. Search for tones which will express the sincerity of the thoughts.

8. *Will Shakespeare,* by Clemence Dane.

Compare Henslowe's speeches in Act III, Scene 1, telling how he saw Anne in Stratford, with his speech in Act I, Scene 1, beginning—

Why, yes and no! I'm from Spain at the moment—I have castles there

The one reveals the man, the other reveals the actor.

9. *Will Shakespeare:* Act II, Scene 1.

Study the dialogue between Queen Elizabeth and Mary Fitton. Note the effect of character and dialogue upon both speed and tone. Frequently players are criticized because one character takes the note from another. If actors would compare the various characters and their individual dramatic purposes, they would readily avoid this.

Compare the dialogue in this scene with that between the same two characters in Act IV. These are excellent passages for the study of tune and speed.

10. *Secrets,* by Rudolf Besier: Act I, from the entrance of John Carlton through the bedroom window.

This is a charming scene of romance and comedy. Speed, phrasing, timing, and tone are important for its interpretation.

11. *The Barretts of Wimpole Street,* by Rudolf Besier: Act IV. Dialogue between Robert Browning and Elizabeth.

This scene is not very dissimilar from that in Act I of *Secrets.* It is magnificent romance. This is a splendid exercise in vocalization—speed, tone, and timing—for both Browning and Elizabeth.

12. *The Barretts of Wimpole Street:* Act II.

The character of Browning is particularly interesting. The author states that Browning's speech is "rapid, voluble, and emphasized by free gestures." Study this scene, and observe how rapid speech exactly suits the character and language of this physical and mental giant.

13. *Mrs. Moonlight*, by Benn W. Levy: Act II, Scene 1. Dialogue between Jane and Percy beginning—

Good afternoon, Percy.

A delightful comedy scene. Tone, phrasing, and speed.

14. *The Skin Game*, by John Galsworthy: Act I. Dialogue between Hillcrist, Mrs. Hillcrist, and Hornblower, beginning—

You promised me you know, not to change the tenancies.

Notice how the language indicates personality and character as forcibly as it informs and argues. By phrasing and by the emphasis of words and phrases, as well as by the selection of tones, character and story will be communicated.

Note also the variety of speed within the speeches of Hornblower to indicate the virility and eagerness of this man.

15. *Call it a Day*, by Dodie Smith: Act I, Scene 1. The whole of this scene makes a splendid exercise in "natural" speech.

16. *Call it a Day:* Act II, Scene 1. Dialogue between Ann and Paul beginning—   More bread and butter.

The character of Ann is especially interesting. Her keen mind, and her complete lack of self-consciousness, are extremely fascinating.

17. *His House in Order*, by Pinero: Act III. Nina's speech beginning—

Oh, I know what upsets Filmer so—why everybody is in such a ferment.

Join this speech with the next three of Nina's speeches.

18. *His House in Order:* Act II. Hilary's speech beginning—

Sir Daniel—Filmer—May I tell you all a little story?

and his next six speeches.

This is rather long, but it is an excellent exercise in sustained narrative. Phrasing and stressing of important words are essential.

19. Exercises for cultivating controlled speech are in the following choruses—

(a) *Abraham Lincoln*, by John Drinkwater. Opening of play. End of Scene 5.

(b) Several choruses in *Murder in the Cathedral*, by T. S. Eliot.

(c) *Singing Sands* and other verse plays by Gordon Bottomley.

(d) Choruses from Sophocles's *Antigone* and other Greek plays.

20. *Richard of Bordeaux*, by Gordon Daviot: Act I, Scene 1. Richard's three speeches beginning—

How can I be patient? I know I have a dreadful temper, but how can I be patient?

21. *The Kingdom of God*, by Sierra, translated by Helen and Harley Granville Barker: Act I. Sister Gracia's two speeches beginning—

Give alms! No . . . no . . . oh no! Where's the good in giving away a little of what you have too much of . . .

CHAPTER V

MOVEMENT: THE BODY

THE visual effect of the actor's body, whether in repose or in motion, is very considerable.

Amateurs generally tend to disregard the importance of the effects produced upon the minds of an audience by careless posture, and by movement lacking in dramatic purpose. Round shoulders, drooping heads, lolling postures, fidgety hands and fingers, toes pointing inwards, restless eyes, and shuffling feet should all be clear pointers to character. Unfortunately, they frequently are not this, but merely the indications of a careless or thoughtless attitude towards acting.

Try to stand in a comfortable and easy position. The body must be neither limp nor taut. It must be relaxed. You should hold the body upright, but not stiff; your knees should be free, but not sagging; your arms should be loose, but not limp; your muscles should be in repose, but not slack; the weight of your body should be poised upon your two feet so that you may move easily and comfortably in any direction without noticeable effort. It is of the greatest importance that you should be able to sit and stand comfortably and at ease.

Some will do this quite easily, but many will find it difficult. For the latter I suggest—

Stand poised on your two feet, with the feet slightly apart and one about two inches in front of the other. Hold your body erect, with every limb straight and taut. Now, without moving your feet, relax slightly, so that your weight is still equally distributed between your two feet, your knees are slightly loose, your hands and arms are just slightly bent and free. Your hands should be a little towards the front of your thighs and resting against them.

You should now be quite comfortable and at the same time ready for movement in any direction. You are not limp, nor

are your muscles taut, yet in such a position you will be
alert and ready to move. When you are standing in this
way you will be still and at rest, but there will be alertness,
life, and vigour in your relaxed posture. You will notice
how simply you can sway the whole body; you will
feel that you can readily move in any direction, and that you
can, at will, bring into action any muscle or limb you wish.

On the cricket field one has often seen Don Bradman,
"Patsy" Hendren, and—that perhaps greatest of all
cricketers—Hobbs, standing in this way. They seemed to
be at rest; they sometimes even gave the impression of
laziness; but at the moment of need they would spring into
action with a vigour and certainty that bode ill for the un-
wary batsman. Great fieldsmen such as these adopted and
cultivated this way of standing because experience has
taught them that thus they are ready for movement in any
direction. Thus they are alert.

Similar alertness is essential on the stage, for the actor,
too, must always be ready to move in any direction and at
any required speed. When you are able to stand poised in
this way, so that you can set your body swaying ever so
slightly, and all your limbs are free to move immediately,
you will have gained something of the suppleness of body
that is required.

From the standing position—

Practise walking in various directions and to various distances.
First take four steps to the front, starting off with your left foot.
In walking keep your muscles relaxed. At first there will be a
tendency to draw up the body and tighten the muscles. This must
be avoided, as only for the interpretation of soldierly characters
do we wish to create the effect of stiff uprightness. To complete
the four steps, you will need to bring the left foot up to the right,
so that you may still balance your body equally upon your two
feet.

Repeat this exercise; starting sometimes with your left foot,
sometimes with your right.

Now try this movement—

Take four steps to the front and then three to the right. Before turning, complete the four steps to the front.

You will notice that, to make the movement to the right, you must start off with the right foot. This is important. Now do the exercise, starting first with your left foot, and then with your right foot, and notice the difference in the distribution of the weight of your body at the moment of turning. In order to turn to the right, the weight of the body must be thrown on to the left foot. When you start with your right foot, the weight naturally falls on your left foot on the fourth step, and thus the turn comes more easily.

Make up similar walking exercises for yourself, and note particularly the importance of correct footwork. Footwork is as important in acting as it is in dancing, tennis, cricket, or boxing. In doing these exercises see that all your muscles are relaxed, and especially that you keep a cheerful facial expression.

Now, again from your original free standing position, try some kneeling exercises—

Kneel on the left knee, then on the right knee. First take a step forward with your right foot and kneel on your left knee. Then change, and take a step forward with your left foot and kneel on your right knee.

Notice where your arms and hands naturally fall.

Keep your back and head in their normal line.

Now—

Kneel on your left knee, but do not move your right foot; and similarly kneel on your right knee, but do not move your left foot. Always keep your back and head in their normal line and again notice the natural position of the arms and hands.

With these kneeling exercises you might combine some arm movements—

As you kneel, lift your arms in supplication, or raise your arm or arms in salutation.

In the former case your hands will face upwards, while in the latter they will be turned downwards.

And how will you kneel? Will you step forward and kneel, or will you step back and kneel on the knee that you move? Is there any emotional difference between these two ways of kneeling, or will it just depend on the room you have on the stage? Perhaps the step forward as you kneel may suggest eagerness and hopefulness, while the withdrawing movement may suggest fear or perhaps awe. Perhaps there will not be a clear demarcation between the significance of these two movements; yet I am sure that you will be sensitive to some psychological and emotional difference which will cause, and direct, selection when occasion arises.

In making these movements you will notice the necessity of co-ordinating the movements of kneeling with the lifting of the arms. They are not two separate movements. They spring from the same emotional, and perhaps rational, urge, and must therefore be one movement, beginning at the same time and finishing at the same time. The arms move upwards as you kneel, and become taut as the movement is completed. In supplication the hands are slightly bent and the fingers slightly curved and apart. In salutation the hands are almost flat with the fingers stretched forward and nearly touching each other, although the thumb will be pointing outwards.

In both these exercises the head and face are also of the greatest importance. In supplication the head is thrown backwards and the eyes look upwards in the direction of the arms. The expression on the face may vary. It will depend upon the emotional stress of the supplication. There may be strain and worry in the expression; there may be happiness and sublime trust. If it is the former, the eyes will be more than half closed, the brow will be furrowed, the arms and fingers will be excessively taut, and the exercise may become an expression of the deepest agony. Thus did King Lear supplicate the heavens, until in the bitterness of his anguish the muscles of his arms and hands drew his fingers into a tightly clenched fist which beat upon his brow the measure and rhythm of his distress.

Arm movements are generally difficult for beginners. It is important that you should develop broad, sweeping movements of the arms. Try the following exercises—

1. *Stand facing the front, with your feet slightly apart, and your right foot about six inches in front of the left. Put nearly all your weight on your right foot. Let the arms lie at rest, relaxed and comfortable, your hands against your thighs. Now raise your right arm forwards and slightly outwards. Keep the arm just slightly relaxed and do not turn it. Move your arm upwards in this way until your hand is nearly over your shoulder. The hand, with the fingers slightly bent, is now facing the front.*

Perform this exercise. It is not a salute. Examine your mental attitude as you do it. If you allow your head to move slightly back and keep your eyes directed in front of you, you will perhaps find yourself saying, "Stop," or "Listen."

Repeat with your left arm.

2. *Stand facing the front, with your feet slightly apart, and your left foot about six inches behind the right. Put nearly all your weight on your right foot. Let the arms lie at rest, relaxed and comfortable, and the hands against the thighs. Now raise the right arm forwards and slightly outwards, keeping the elbow and the fingers slightly bent. As the arm reaches the level of the shoulder let the hand turn so that it is facing inwards. Now let the arm move upwards until it is about nine inches above the level of the shoulder and let your hand turn upwards as you raise your arm.*

Repeat with the left arm.

3. *Place your left hand on your hip and stand facing the front, with your feet slightly apart and your left foot about six inches behind the right. Place the weight of your body on your left foot.*

Bring the right hand across the body so that the index finger nearly touches the knuckles of the left hand, and keep the right elbow well out in front of the body. All the fingers should be slightly curved, and the thumb of the right hand should lightly touch the body. Now with a sweeping movement swing the right arm across the body and slightly upwards until it points diagonally outwards towards the right. As you swing the arm, keep the palm of the hand facing downwards, stretch the index finger, keep the other fingers bent, the thumb stretched outwards, and transfer the weight of the body to the right foot. Your head should move round in the direction of your hand.

When you have mastered this exercise, the movement of the right hand across the body towards the left hand, and then across the body towards the right, should be done in one complete movement with no apparent break.

Repeat this movement, slowly and then quickly, and sometimes with relaxed muscles and then with all the muscles tightened.

While you are performing this exercise, examine your mental attitude and feelings. Note especially your feelings as your muscles tighten and your arm sweeps rapidly across your body. What do you want to say as you make this movement? Perhaps, "Begone! Run to your houses!"

4. *Perform Exercise 3 again; only this time, as you swing your right arm forward and outwards, make a step forward with your right foot.*

5. Stand as in Exercise 3—

Bring the right arm across the body so that the right elbow is well out in front of the body, and the index finger is pointing towards the left elbow. Keep the fingers slightly bent and swing the arm across the body towards the right. Keep the palm of the hand facing downwards and finish with the hand slightly above the shoulder. Repeat the movement, and now turn the hand as you swing the arm so that the palm faces upwards.

Repeat this movement, starting from various heights; sometimes at the elbow and sometimes with the right hand on the level of the left shoulder.

In all these exercises be sure that the elbow of the moving arm is well away from the body.

6. *Stand at rest. Raise both arms forward together until the hands are level with your shoulders, keeping the palms of the hands facing downwards and keeping all muscles slightly relaxed.*

7. *Stand at rest with the right foot slightly in front of the left. This time, as you raise your arms forward, turn the hands inwards so that, when they are level with the shoulders, the palms will be facing upwards. Notice that, as the hands come up, the whole body naturally tends to sway forward and the weight is thrown more upon the right foot. Keep the fingers slightly bent.*

8. *Perform Exercise 7 again. This time, however, as your hands reach the level of your shoulders, take a lunging step forward with your right foot, throw nearly all the weight of your body on the right foot, but keep your balance by the slight pressure of your left foot on the ground. As you make the step forward, tighten the shoulder and upper arm muscles. This will cause your elbow to bend slightly.*

Again, as you perform this exercise, examine your mental attitude. Can you not speak your thoughts as you make this movement? This was the movement used in Granville-Barker's production of *Twelfth Night* by Sebastian and Viola as they faced each other in Act V, each uncertain of the other's reality, yet eager to embrace.

Make up exercises of your own to develop free and curving movements. Make sweeping greetings with a hat, fling a cloak about your shoulders in one sweeping movement. Do anything which will help you to develop free, easy, and comfortable arm and body movements.

Ability to sit comfortably is also essential. Many people find it extremely difficult to sit and keep a straight back. The bent back and round shoulders have a most disastrous effect. Others, when sitting, have no idea where to put their hands, and they allow these to fidget hither and thither like birds trying to find a resting place. Practise sitting in various postures, and always have a definite position for your hands. Make up your mind whether you will put your hands in your lap, on your knees, or perhaps one resting on a knee, the other on your hip. Try various positions. Fold your arms, or let them hang limply by your side. Examine the various positions, and think about the effect each would make.

Practise sitting down and getting up. Frequently these apparently simple tasks cause considerable trouble on the stage. In ordinary life we make no trouble of such a task because it does not really matter how we do it. But on the stage, when we wish to preserve some kind of dignity or purpose, it is a matter that calls for care. Again, the chief difficulty is usually with the back. Many people find it almost impossible to sit down without doubling themselves up, or else they go to the other extreme and sit down as if they were wearing a back-board.

Always you must consider the effect your way of sitting or standing will have upon your audience. You will not look like a soldier just because you are in a uniform, and an Empire frock may look like a sack of potatoes tied about the middle unless you stand, sit, and move in a becoming manner.

Miming exercises are of considerable value in developing free and co-ordinated movements of the body. It is important, however, to remember that miming exercises should be a test of your ability to communicate ideas by movement. They should not be used as memory tests. You should observe carefully so that you may prepare an appropriate sequence of actions. If necessary, write down each separate movement, and build up your mime from your notes. Mime should follow deliberate observation. Observe, record, and build up accurate mental images of actions, and draw upon these images for your interpretation. It is your aim, in performing a mime, to convey a story by action to an audience. Each detail must be clear and must give precise information,

Try the following mimes—

1. *A bill-poster posting a poster on a hoarding.*
2. *A butcher scraping and scrubbing a table.*
3. *A grocer making up a parcel of a number of purchases for a customer.*
4. *A lady purchasing a hat.*
5. *A lady receives a box. She opens it and discovers roses sent by a friend. She places these in two vases, one of which she puts on the mantelpiece and the other on an occasional table.*

Some points to be observed in all these mimes are: actions, sizes of objects, distances, and speed.

Mime the following stories—

1. *A little girl takes her doll from its cot. She undresses it and gives it a bath. She puts on its night attire and puts it to bed.*
2. *Bassanio is before the caskets of lead, silver, and gold. These he examines. He rejects the gold and silver caskets and finally chooses the leaden one. In it he finds a picture of Portia and a scroll which tells him what to do. It tells him to "go to where thy lady is, and claim her with a loving kiss."*
3. *You enter a room. You do not wish to be disturbed or over-looked. You are in search of an important document. You examine every part of the writing desk. You turn to a bureau; at last you find what you are seeking between two books in a bookcase. You hurry away with the document.*
4. *You are eagerly waiting for the postman to arrive. He brings you a letter, which contains exciting news. You hurriedly dress and go out.*
5. *You are rehearsing a part for a play. The part you are rehearsing is where you have to present a special petition to the King in his Throne Room.*

Make up miming exercises of your own—exercises that will compel you to practise walking, sitting, kneeling, and movements with the hands. Mime parts of scenes from any play you may be reading.

SUMMARY

1. The visual effect of the actor's person, whether in repose or in motion, is very considerable.
2. The body in repose.
3. Alertness is essential on the stage.
4. Exercises in walking.
5. Exercises in walking and turning.
6. Exercises in kneeling.
7. Exercises in kneeling and arm movements.
8. Importance of the position of the head and the expression on the face.
9. Arm movements.
10. Ability to sit comfortably is essential.
11. The value of miming exercises.
12. Some miming exercises.

EXERCISES ON CHAPTER V

1. *The Happy Journey*, by Thornton Wilder.

An unusual play and one which presents many problems for those interested in mime. The audience watch the Kirby family make a journey in a car made of four chairs on an otherwise empty stage. It is "make believe" at its best and demands the closest discipline in team co-ordination.

2. *My Lady's Dress*, by Edward Knoblock.

The Dutch scene in this play provides excellent study in stylized and elegant movement; so in the ultra-fashionable showroom of Jacquelin's salon there is a mannequin parade which provides several ladies with opportunity for detailed study of deportment and the art of walking.

CHAPTER VI

GESTURE

SOME years ago I took a party of boys to Shanklin. We arrived in the early afternoon on a beautiful sunny day. We walked from the station down the road leading to the sea. As we reached the brow of the hill, a boy suddenly stopped, stood still, and gazed out towards the expanse of glittering blue. His face and eyes were aglow with wonder. Slowly he lifted his hand and pointed. Quietly he asked: "Is that the sea?"

Gesture must spring from thought, and usually it precedes speech.

Try some simple exercises—

(a) *You see a beautiful landscape in the distance. You point it out to a friend.*

Observe the sequence of action—

1. *You see the landscape and your face and eyes express your sense of joy and wonder.*
2. *Your hand comes up to point towards the scene.*
3. *You exclaim: "Look! Isn't it beautiful?"*

Oh no, that won't do. You show that you are entirely unmoved. Your gesture must spring from your thoughts. It is not enough for you to see and feel. Your face must express your feelings to me, your audience. Try again. As you observe the landscape, open your eyes wide and gaze intently. Let your whole face express the ecstasy of your emotion. From this emotion your gesture must grow.

Yes, I can see that you appreciate what you have to do; but now you must see to it that your speech is in sympathy with your facial expression and with your arm movement. The "timing" of the speech with the movement is important. Although speech follows gesture, it does not lag far behind. In fact as the gesture is completed you must begin to speak.

(*b*) *On the table are several pictures. You are looking at them. Suddenly you see one that is very beautiful and by your favourite painter.*

Work out the sequence of action—

1. *You are looking at this collection of pictures, first at one and then at another.*

2. *You see one that appeals especially to you. Your face lights up with joy.*

3. *You move towards this picture, eagerly. Perhaps your hands go out to pick it up.*

4. *Your body is tense with excitement and you exclaim— "Isn't this one lovely ! It's by Millais, isn't it ?"*

Now don't be so blasé ! IF YOU ARE EVER GOING TO ACT, YOU MUST BE ABLE TO EXPRESS GREAT EMOTION, EVEN THOUGH YOU DON'T FEEL IT.

(*c*) *Your little girl is standing sobbing over a broken doll. You console her by saying: " My darling, don't cry."*

Picture this little scene. Act it and find gesture which will emphasize your sympathy.

Sequence of action—

1. *You look down at your little girl, and your face expresses your sympathy. Perhaps a suspicion of a smile plays around your lips.*

2. *Your hand goes out towards her. The palm of your hand will, I think, be facing downwards, for you are probably preparing to stroke your little girl's head.*

3. *As your hand reaches her head you say as sympathetically as possible: " My darling, don't cry."*

Oh, yes, I am aware that you could be cross when saying this; but then your gesture would be different, and "my darling" would signify the reverse. All right, if you feel that way, act it as if you are angry, and make the appropriate gesture.

This exercise will perhaps suggest that most charming episode in *Dear Brutus* when Lob talks to his flowers after they have dropped on the floor.

(d) *Take up your copy of "Dear Brutus," turn to this passage in Act I, and try to follow the movements and expressions of dear old Lob.*

He sees the flowers at his feet where they have dropped from the bowl that is in his hands. His face shows his distress; one hand moves from the bowl as if it would soothe those hurt flowers, slowly he kneels, puts the bowl down beside him. Gently—oh, ever so gently—he picks up one of his darling flowers, and hugs it to him. His face moves closer to the flower, his head moves from side to side, and then he gently places it on the floor as he turns to another.

Proceed right through the speech, fitting gestures to accompany each thought and each expression. Take care that every movement has a definite purpose and that throughout proper regard is given to Lob's age and his sensitiveness to the feelings and understanding of the flowers he is talking to.

This is a difficult speech. The gesture is difficult to control and to communicate as being the natural result of thought and feeling: but do try it, over and over again. You will not master it the first time, nor the second, nor the third. Try each little bit separately until each little gesture seems right to you, and, sincerely, the result of a feeling created within you. Practise it with any objects, toy, or creature that you like. Practise picking up these and talking to them as if they do really understand what you are saying, as if they do respond to your affection. When you have mastered this speech, with its appropriate gesture, you will have made tremendous progress in the art of acting.

(e) *Turn to "Dear Brutus," Act II—the entrance of Margaret and Dearth. Try to create gesture for Margaret's two speeches.*

In the first of these it is not so much a question of gesture as one of posture, of exaggerated pose—playfully "taking off" the picture critic. The second speech calls for more true gesture, again somewhat exaggerated to poke fun at her daddy as he may sometimes appear in his studio. In your

study of these two speeches, try to get at the impish thoughts
which call forth the words. These thoughts will suggest
gestures. Then think the thought, and follow it up with the
gesture and the words.

(*f*) *Get down your copy of "Macbeth." Turn to Act II,
Scene* 1—*the famous "Dagger" speech.*

Macbeth has just sent a servant off to bid his mistress strike
the bell when his drink is ready. He is thinking of the foul
deed he is to commit, and fancies that he sees a dagger
before him. He speaks—

> Is this a dagger which I see before me,
> The handle toward my hand? Come, let me clutch thee:
> I have thee not, and yet I see thee still.

A gesture is clearly imposed by Shakespeare, yet it is one
that is most difficult to make convincing. Macbeth's mind
is distraught with the horror of what he is about to do. His
imagination fools him. He thinks he sees that which he
knows cannot be there. He questions the reality because
his reason quarrels with his senses. His mind is already fearful; as he looks upon his vision of a dagger his face reveals
his terror and also his scepticism. He speaks as his hand
hesitantly comes up towards the object that appears to be
there. When his hand is nearly touching this thing, he makes
to clutch it and speaks the words—

> Come, let me clutch thee.

This action of clutching must be achieved in such a manner
that, if he were successful, he would have it in the hand ready
to strike. The action is completed just before the words are
finished. Then at once he feels an empty hand, but still
may see the dagger beyond his hand. Tightly he clenches the
uplifted fist, gazes fearfully at the dagger beyond, and with
the greatest dread, and in almost a whisper utters the
terrible paradox—

> I have thee not, and yet I see thee still.

Try it yourself: the clenching of the fist, done with such

intensity of emotion that you will perhaps be trembling as Macbeth undoubtedly was.

All these exercises indicate the importance of facial expression. Indeed, FACIAL EXPRESSION MUST BE REGARDED AS AN ESSENTIAL PART OF GESTURE.

In ordinary life facial expression, or the lack of it, is frequently a barrier behind which we hide our thoughts. On the stage the face must never hide thoughts from the audience; its expression must be controlled to illuminate thoughts and emotions.

Generally speaking, inexperienced actors are too earnest in their endeavours before an audience. They appear too serious. They mistake looking serious and thoughtful for giving expression to thoughts. You have no doubt listened to amateur choirs. They are so eager to sing well, they try so hard, that as they sing, say, *Merrie England* they look as if they were in a dentist's waiting-room.

YOU MUST LEARN TO SMILE. You must be able to look pleased. You must cultivate control of your eyes, to open them wide, to look out of the corners, to look down, to look puzzled, and so on. Above all, I repeat, DO LEARN TO SMILE. I have known so many students who simply could not smile when once they got on to a stage. Many others have thought that they were smiling when actually they looked as if they would burst into tears at any moment. You must exaggerate.

Let us try some exercises—

1. *The curtain goes up. You are sitting on the stage. You recall an episode that makes you smile. Suddenly you realize that you have an appointment. You get up and go out. The curtain comes down.*

Make yourself comfortable as you sit on the stage, and let your audience see you thinking before you smile. Please exaggerate the smile, so that those a long way from the stage will see it. Let the smile go rapidly as you think of your appointment. Perhaps you will look at your watch or a clock. You will rise hurriedly, put on a hat and perhaps a coat, and quickly go from the room. Remember the door.

2. *The curtain goes up. You are on the stage reading a letter. The letter contains news that is very sad, but concludes with a narrative that is amusing. The curtain comes down.*

Be careful in this exercise to separate completely the second part from the first. Perhaps you will pause to think over the first part before you pass on to the more cheerful ending. Try to let the audience realize that you have come to the end of the letter.

3. *The curtain goes up. You have several pictures on a table. One of these is a delightful picture of a place you know well, another is a humorous cartoon, a third is a portrait of a dear friend, a fourth is a picture of a pit disaster. You look at these in turn. The curtain comes down.*

4. *Turn to your copy of "Dear Brutus," Act I. Play the part of any one of the ladies on the stage when Matey enters for the first time.*

You will realize that at this point of this scene each of the ladies is anxiously wanting to see how Matey conducts himself, but is at the same time pretending to be very much occupied with other business.

In this exercise you will have opportunity of practising looking out of the corners of your eyes, without moving your head.

5. *The curtain goes up. You are reading a passage from a letter which makes you very angry. You get more and more angry the more you read. When you have finished the letter you are "boiling with rage." The curtain comes down.*

6. *The curtain goes up. You are reading a book which is very funny. It gets funnier and funnier. The climax causes you to burst into uncontrolled laughter. The curtain comes down.*

In this exercise you see the phrase: "uncontrolled

laughter." It is of very great importance that you should realize that on the stage this laughter will be very much controlled. Yet it will have to appear to be uncontrolled.

In all the exercises you have been asked to perform you will have noticed the importance of accurate "timing" between thought, gesture, and speech. TIMING IS A SUBTLE QUALITY OF ACTING WHICH MORE THAN ANYTHING ELSE CONVEYS A SENSE OF TRUTH AND SINCERITY.

The application of gesture is at once fascinating and elusive.

It was customary, in an age not very far remote, for gesture to be almost entirely conventionalized; for each emotion to be represented by its own special gesture of hands, head, and eyes. And we may still read textbooks in which gestures are suggested to accompany almost every phrase of a speech. Such methods of interpretation no longer obtain. Instead we may often observe a complete lack of gesture. The revolt against purely artificial and exaggerated gesture has led, in many cases, to an equally exaggerated and illogical suppression of gesture.

GESTURE AND MOVEMENT MUST ALWAYS BE REGARDED AS ESSENTIAL ELEMENTS OF DRAMATIC PRESENTATION. They distinguish the stage picture from a painting. They are natural parts of the lives of the characters of drama. Indeed, the natural gesture of some characters is as memorable as the language they speak.

What has Sir James Barrie to tell us about gesture? Take from your shelf Barrie's *The Admirable Crichton*. Turn to Act III. As you know, circumstances have brought about a reversal in the social positions of the characters. The aristocrats of Act I have become the "hewers of wood and the drawers of water" in Act III; the leader and ruler of the shipwrecked party was, in other days, the butler serving those who now obey him. In this act Barrie tells us that the aristocrats have assumed gestures which rightly belong to the servants' hall. Crichton admonishes Mary for "that action of the hands," "like one washing them." He has forgotten that he used to do it when he was a butler.

At the end of this act Barrie again gives instruction with regard to gesture. Of Crichton he writes: *"By an effort of will he ceases to be an erect figure; he has the humble bearing of a servant. His hands come together as if he were washing them."*

In Act I of this play Lady Mary is described as indolent and languorous, her movements as slow and haughty, her gesture as leisurely and infrequent. In Act III Barrie describes this same young lady as "tingling with vitality," her movements as "deft" and "noiseless." He tells us she leaps through the window and we hear her whistling.

All this indicates an intimacy between gesture and character. CHARACTER IMPOSES GESTURE ON AN ACTOR.

You may have read that gestures must be perfectly natural to the actor himself. The foregoing would seem to enforce the truth that AN ACTOR MUST SELECT GESTURES NATURAL TO THE CHARACTER, AND THEN BY PRACTICE MAKE THEM APPEAR NATURAL TO HIMSELF.

In Granville-Barker's production of *Twelfth Night*, in Act V both Viola and Sebastian used a similar gesture and adopted a similar posture because each was moved by a similar emotional impulse. Both raised their arms to the level of their shoulders, with the palms of the hands facing upwards and with the fingers slightly bent, as they took a step forward and put the weight of the body on the front foot. (As in Exercise 8 in Chapter V.) Turn to this scene in your copy of *Twelfth Night*. Rehearse this episode between Viola and Sebastian, beginning with Sebastian's—

Do I stand there?

Notice how the movements and gestures exactly interpret the innermost hopes of each and emphasize the yearning love of this brother and sister. An important feature in this episode, as produced by Granville-Barker, was that the gesture was held just as long as the emotion lasted; that is, from the moment they saw each other down to when Viola says—

That I am Viola.

the gesture was held because the emotion demanded it. These twins, alike in every physical feature, suffered emotion as like as their features, and this twin gesture added to the illusion.

I am not suggesting that, night after night, during that very long run, Miss Lillah McCarthy and Mr. Dennis Neilson-Terry felt this emotion throughout the scene. It really does not matter what they felt. What I am stating is that this gesture, combined with their speech, compelled the audience to feel the emotional urge uniting Viola and Sebastian.

In this scene we observe an intimacy between gesture and emotion. THE EMOTION OF A CHARACTER IMPOSES GESTURE ON AN ACTOR; AND THE GESTURE WILL LAST JUST AS LONG AS THE EMOTION LASTS.

But there is another important lesson to be learned from this episode. It is sometimes said that gesture is the natural result of emotional feeling. In some cases this may be true. But surely it would be stretching credulity too far to ask us to believe that both Miss McCarthy and Mr. Neilson-Terry were moved to express their own emotional feeling in exactly the same way. Is it not more credible that *a way was agreed upon* by which both at the same time and in the same way were able to achieve a desired objective?

Again, we see that ACTORS MUST SELECT GESTURE AND BY PRACTICE MAKE IT APPEAR TO BE THE NATURAL RESULT OF EMOTION.

It is perhaps a pity that we cannot watch the performances of great actors and actresses of the past, to learn from them how they used gesture to assist them in their interpretations.

Fortunately, we have recorded for us, scene by scene, the performance of *Hamlet* by John Gielgud. Miss Rosamond Gilder has done this for us, and I advise all students of acting to read and study this volume.[1] As you read the record of what was done in this production, you will observe the care that was taken with regard to gesture and business to bring out essential characteristics of important characters and also important details of the play. You will observe how the gesture of one character may affect the gesture of another—

> The Queen goes up to Claudius with a placating gesture and, turning towards Hamlet, begins her plea to him to remain at Elsinore. As she speaks she leans against the King, an *intimate gesture which makes her son's eyes drop*. (The italics are mine.)

In this episode, the gesture of the Queen has nothing to do with the words she is speaking; it is in no way to emphasize her language, nor does it spring from any immediate emotion. It is just a simple and natural gesture of a wife towards her husband. Of itself it is almost insignificant, but in its setting and in relation to Hamlet at this particular time it is a gesture of considerable import. It directs attention to Hamlet's attitude towards his mother's marriage. The actor here has deliberately created gesture to assist him in the achievement of his purpose.

Here is an interesting passage by John Gielgud himself—

> I do not know whether I invented or acquired from someone else the business of seeing the Ghost from the expression of Horatio's face and then turning slowly and looking at it before "Angels and ministers of grace," *but I do know that this came off very well in London. For some reason I could not make it so convincing in New York.* I have never written on the tablets, because I could not manage them and a pencil and a sword all at the same time. I have always used "the table of my memory" and banged my head at "So, uncle, there you are." *Schoolchildren always thought this funny, and I had to cut it (or do it very quietly) at matinées.*

[1] *John Gielgud's Hamlet*, by Rosamond Gilder (Methuen).

The italics are mine, for I would particularly have you note that gesture must communicate its intention to the audience. On the amateur stage, in particular, we may often observe gesture which in itself is appropriate enough from the point of view of character and emotion, but which fails completely to convey its intention to the audience. It does not "get over," as the actor would say.

Always the purpose of the actor is to reveal and make clear his text and his character to the audience. Gesture is employed to interpret and reveal character, to emphasize and communicate emotion, and to direct attention to particular moments of interest. The relation of gesture to the audience must always be in the mind of an actor.

It has frequently been stated that you should make a gesture only when you feel compelled to do so. Up to a point there is much sense in this, but with inexperienced actors I have not found it very useful, nor do the foregoing examples lend support to its truth. It seems to me that this presupposes that the actor has already assumed the personality and mentality of the character he is playing. Unfortunately, however, this is very rare. Only great actors achieve this consistently: good actors do so sometimes, and the majority of us who try to act, but very seldom. And, even if the actor has achieved this, there is still the need to make the gestures acceptable to an audience.

Appropriate gestures will very rarely come to you naturally, or as a result of feeling. Gesture must be considered rationally. You must consider the purpose of your character and your speech, and create gestures to aid you in your objective. THERE SHOULD BE REASON FOR EVERY GESTURE YOU MAKE, AND YOU SHOULD PRACTISE YOUR GESTURES UNTIL THEY APPEAR TO BE NATURAL AND SPONTANEOUS.

The plays of Shakespeare may provide you with an abundance of opportunities for the study of gesture. In *The Merchant of Venice* we have the Prince of Morocco, the Prince of Arragon, and Bassanio all separately choosing

from the caskets. Here are three distinct characters whose
object is identical. Work out gestures which will be appropriate for their individual characters, which will reveal the
emotional aspect of each, and which will convey the purpose of each scene.

In Act III, Scene 2, of the same play, Bassanio is reading
the letter which tells him of Antonio's failure to repay his
debt to Shylock. Portia watches Bassanio as he reads and
says—

> There are some shrewd contents in yon same paper,
> That steals the colour from Bassanio's cheek;
> Some dear friend dead; else nothing in the world
> Could turn so much the constitution
> Of any constant man. What, worse and worse !—
> With leave, Bassanio; I am half yourself,
> And I must freely have the half of anything
> That this same paper brings you.

Think out gesture which will reveal Portia's growing
emotion during the first part of this speech, and appropriate
movement and gesture as she makes her appeal to share
with Bassanio the burden of the letter.

Men will find many interesting studies in *Julius Caesar* and
Henry V—studies which will give them opportunities for
broad gesture as well as delicate and subtle gesture. Turn
to the famous "Harfleur" speech in Act III, Scene 1, of
Henry V. Speak this speech, and find gesture that will help
you to give emphasis to the character of Henry, his thoughts,
and his emotions. This is a speech of dramatic movement
and stirring power. It is one in which gesture may be appropriately used, for it springs from the need for action, urges
action, and is spoken by a man of action.

Picture in your mind this King Henry standing before
his dejected and weary men, urging them on to greater effort
and greater deeds. See him standing erect and bold, eager
and vigorous. He knows that immediate and speedy action
is a necessity. Is he not standing firmly poised upon his
two feet? Perhaps his right foot is slightly in front of the

left, his left hand rests firmly upon the hilt of his sword. Rapidly his speech moves on, as enthusiasm and impatience for action invigorate his whole body. Speak the speech and tighten your muscles and stretch your body to its fullest height as you say—

> . . . and bend up every spirit
> To his full height.

Raise your arm above your head as you cry—

> On, on you, noble English,

just as you did in Exercise 3 in Chapter V. Study this Exercise again, and also Exercise 4. Try the movement with this speech, and I think you will find it appropriate as you speak—

> On, on, you noble English,
> Whose blood is fet from fathers of war-proof!
> Fathers, that like so many Alexanders,
> Have in these parts from morn till even fought,
> And sheathed their swords for lack of argument.

Feel the muscles of the arm get taut and strained as the hand moves to emphasize the repeated word "Fathers." And I think you will want to bring the arm down and back across your body towards the hilt of your sword, in order to imitate the action of sheathing your sword on the last line.

In this speech, I feel, gesture is needed to suit the words and also to emphasize the emotion, or—should we not say?— to carry over the emotional need for action into the hearts of the soldiers and the audience.

Read Act II of *Pygmalion*. Here we have a group of very distinctive characters—distinctive as much by reason of gesture as anything else. Professor Higgins, Colonel Pickering, and Doolittle; Eliza and Mrs. Pearce. Think of them as physical human beings. Think of the three men as they converse together in the Professor's laboratory. Picture in your mind the irascible and eccentric Professor, the retired Indian Army Colonel, and the Cockney dustman. Stand as they stand, walk as they walk, and create gestures which will be appropriate for each of these very different characters. Treat Eliza and Mrs. Pearce in the same way.

Take the three speeches of Professor Higgins, beginning—

What is life but a series of follies

and ending with

Wrap her up in brown paper till they come.

Treat them as one speech. Create gesture for them. This is a lovely moment.

Closely associated with gesture is "*stage business.*" Actually it is gesture with a special application. Frequently such business is imposed upon the actor by the author himself. In *Pygmalion*, Act II, the dialogue indicates that Professor Higgins shall cut a chocolate in half, eat one half himself and give the other half to Eliza. This particular piece of business may be very effective and very funny. From the text we may realize that Eliza does not trust Higgins, and that she would certainly not eat any of the chocolate of her own free will. The chocolate must somehow be forced upon her. This business will appear perfectly natural, and will achieve the purpose of the scene, if Eliza turns her head towards Higgins and speaks her habitual "garn." Exactly at that moment Higgins pops one half of the chocolate into his own mouth and the other into hers. When this is "timed" absolutely accurately it "brings the house down."

Sir James Barrie was very fond indeed of introducing business into his plays. Accurate timing with the bucket business in *The Admirable Crichton* makes this always an effective source of laughter. And the wrapping up of the missing Miss Livy in Act IV of *Quality Street* is a wonderful piece of business when Valentine Brown takes the proper care to mime it with accuracy in every detail.

Practise any piece of business you can find in the plays you know. It is an excellent way of becoming skilled not only in movement and gesture, but also in the art of correct and effective timing.

Stage business is not always imposed by the dramatist.

Actors have always been fond of introducing business of their own. Sometimes the business is legitimate, but I regret to say that often it is unwarranted interpolation. Naturally, the plays of Shakespeare and the older dramatists lend themselves more readily to the introduction of business by the actors than do modern plays. This is so because the older playwrights gave fewer instructions to the actors. In the modern play the text is frequently so loaded with directions that little room is left for the actor to invent. This is sometimes good, but at times it is very bad. Not all dramatists have such a fine sense of the stage as Barrie and Shaw. Barrie, in particular, is almost uncanny in his sense of business that will be effective.

One of the finest pieces of stage business the theatre has given us for many a day was that invented by John Gielgud in his production of *Hamlet*. Hamlet found the King's sword lying on the chair while the King was at prayer. He took it up and carried it with him into the Queen's chamber, and it was thus with the King's sword that he killed Polonius. It was a piece of business that naturally developed from the action of the play, and gave a sense of fitness to the scenes that followed.

This should be the test of business. It should always spring naturally from the action of the play itself, and be appropriate to the characters doing it, and it should at the same time illuminate some aspect of the play or the characters.

SUMMARY

1. **Gesture must spring from thought, and usually it precedes speech.**

2. **You must be able to express great emotion, even though you do not feel it.**

3. **Facial expression must be regarded as an essential part of gesture.**

4. **You must learn to smile.**

5. **Timing is a subtle quality of acting which more than anything else conveys a sense of truth and sincerity.**

6. **Gesture and movement must be regarded as essential elements of dramatic presentation.**

7. **Character imposes gesture on an actor.**

8. **An actor must select gestures natural to the character, and then by practice make them appear natural to himself.**

9. **The emotion of a character imposes gesture on an actor.**

10. **The gesture will last just as long as the emotion lasts.**

11. **Actors must select gesture and by practice make it appear to be the natural result of emotion.**

12. *John Gielgud's Hamlet*, **by Rosamond Gilder.**

13. **Gesture must communicate its intention to the audience.**

14. **The purpose of the actor is to reveal and make clear his text and his character to the audience.**

15. **There should be reason for every gesture you make, and you should practise your gestures until they appear to be natural and spontaneous.**

16. **Stage business is closely associated with gesture.**

17. **Stage business is sometimes imposed by the dramatist, and frequently it is created by the actor.**

EXERCISES ON CHAPTER VI

1. *Antigone*, by Sophocles (Elsie Fogerty's Edition).

Gesture and movement are important and essential for all Greek plays.

Create gesture for Antigone's speech near the opening of the play beginning—

> What! Hath not Kreon doomed our brothers twain,
> One to an honoured burial, one to shame?

Compare the gesture appropriate for this speech with that suitable for Kreon's speech in the first episode beginning—

> People of Thebes! The gods who guide our state,
> After long tossing on the waves of strife,
> Once more have steadied it in wonted course.

2. *A Midsummer Night's Dream:* Act II, Scene 1. Puck's speech beginning—

> Thou speak'st aright,
> I am that merry wanderer of the night.

Puck is a sophisticated and mischievous spirit, and can best be interpreted by a man who is not too tall or too big.

Also Act III, Scene 2. Puck's speech beginning—

> My mistress with a monster is in love.

Both these speeches need quick movement and gesture.

3. *A Midsummer Night's Dream:* Act II, Scene 2. Titania's speech beginning—

> Come, now a roundel and a fairy song.

Graceful arm movements.

Also, Act III, Scene 1. Titania's speech beginning—
> Out of this wood do not desire to go.

4. *Julius Caesar:* Act I, Scene 1. Marullus's speech—
> Wherefore rejoice? What conquest brings he home?

Big arm movements and taut, strained limbs.

5. *Julius Caesar:* Act III, Scene 1. Antony's speech—
> O, pardon me, thou bleeding piece of earth.

Kneeling. Hand and arm movements.

6. *Twelfth Night:* Act II, Scene 5. Malvolio's speech—
> M.O.A.I.—this simulation is not as the former.

Posture. Grotesque movement of limbs, enforced unnatural smiling.

7. *Hamlet:* Act III, Scene 1. Hamlet's soliloquy—
> To be, or not to be—that is the question.

Head movement—eyes. Movement about the stage.

8. *Hamlet:* Act III, Scene 1. Hamlet's speeches to the players.
Gesture of arms, and movements of the whole body, are needed to stress certain comments.

9. *Macbeth:* Act V, Scene 1. Lady Macbeth's sleep-walking speeches.
Walking and hand movements.

10. *Macbeth:* Act II, Scene 3. The Porter's speech—
> Here's a knocking indeed.

Drunken movement and gesture. Miming.

11. *King Lear:* Act II, Scene 4. Lear's speech—
> O, reason not the need; our basest beggars
> Are in poorest thing superfluous.

Note: Comedy of manners demands elegance of movement and gesture of a specialized kind. Men need to cultivate wrist movements, manner of snuff-taking, walking, and bowing. Ladies manipulate the fan with dexterity, and curtsy with grace and charm.

12. *The School for Scandal:* Act II, Scene 2.
The whole of this scene makes an excellent exercise for the study and practice of elegant walking, bowing, curtsying, delicate movements of the hands, head, and feet, the use of the snuff-box, handkerchief, and fan.

13. *The School for Scandal:* Act III, Scene 3.
In contrast to the former scene with its elegancies and pedantries, this scene shows the free, bold movement of Charles Surface and his friends, and the easy, natural poise of Sir Oliver Surface.

These two scenes, taken together and contrasted, may provide many valuable exercises in movement, gesture, and deportment.

14. *Berkeley Square*, by John Balderston.
An interesting play for its contrasts in movement and gesture.

The Duchess of Devonshire is a model of grace and elegance.

Peter is awkward in his attempts to assume the polish of his eighteenth-century cousins.

Perhaps the most interesting contrast is that between Kate and her sister Helen. Kate displays the elegance and vigour of her period, while Helen, who is spiritually in advance of her time, moves with the simple dignity and poise of a twentieth-century young lady.

15. *Berkeley Square:* Act I, Scene 3. Dialogue between Helen and Peter, beginning—

Won't you sit down, cousin?

Throughout this dialogue the movement is quiet and restful. These two kindred spirits are at peace together.

16. *Berkeley Square:* Act II, Scene 2. Dialogue between Kate and Peter, beginning—

Kate, what's the matter? You've been avoiding me all the evening.

Contrast the movement and gesture of this scene with those of the former. Restlessness of the mind compels movement and gesture.

17. *Berkeley Square:* Act III, Scene 3. Dialogue between Tom and Kate, beginning—

Gad's life! You!

Movement in this episode is vigorous and gesture free.

18. *The Skin Game,* by John Galsworthy: Act I, Scene 1, beginning—

Good morning! good morning! How are ye, Dawker? Fine morning! Lovely weather!

The dialogue between Hillcrist and Hornblower provides a fine contrast between the squire and the self-made industrialist. Gesture is imposed by the characters of Hillcrist and Hornblower, and it gives indication of their respective social background.

19. *Elizabeth Refuses,* by Margaret Macnamara.

A charming one-act comedy which illustrates the witty irony of Jane Austen. This splendid play provides material for the study of both speech and movement.

20. *Square Pegs,* by Clifford Bax.

A "polite satire" in verse for two ladies—the one a modern girl, the other a sixteenth-century Venetian. This is a charming duologue suitable for two young girls or older ladies. Excellent for the study of speech and contrasting movement.

21. *The Lady with a Lamp,* by Reginald Berkeley: Act III, Scene 5. Dialogue between Elizabeth Herbert and Florence Nightingale beginning—

Well,—that's better. Now we can talk—frankly.

Movement and gesture in this scene are dignified, but they respond to the rising emotion of Florence and the fierce antagonism between the two protagonists.

22. *The Only Jealousy of Emer*, by W. B. Yeats.

The curtain bearing and curtain folding at the opening and ending might make an excellent study of controlled and rhythmic walking.

23. *Singing Sands*, by Gordon Bottomley.

The chorus of eight women must acquire graceful movement; they must learn to move rhythmically, with controlled, flowing movements that immediately suggest the waves upon the seashore.

This is a lovely play for women to study and perform. Its lyrical verse is beautiful to speak, while the study of movement for the characters as well as for the chorus is especially fascinating.

24. *The Kingdom of God*, by Sierra. Act III. The speeches of Juan De Dios, the bull-fighter, beginning—

D'you hear that . . . d'you hear that?

and also the speeches following, in which he describes and mimes a bull-fight.

CHAPTER VII

INTERPRETATION

DRAMA is concerned with characters. In reading a play one must strive to perceive more than the mere story and the meaning of the words. One must be eager to see the characters with the mind's eye, and to hear them with the mind's ear.

Modern dramatists supply, in the printed editions of their plays, much that was omitted in Shakespeare's time. The reading public puts much money into the pockets of the modern playwright. To encourage and assist the reader, ample descriptions are given of the scenic background, and considerable explanations are added to the text.

Read for yourself Barrie's introduction to Act I of *Quality Street*. Here he sketches Quality Street itself, the general aspect of the houses, and in particular the Blue and White Room in which the main incidents of the play are to take place. But he does much more than this. He tells us what is happening outside the house when the curtain goes up and the play is about to begin; he describes the ladies of the play for us and tells us exactly what they are doing.

Now these things are very interesting, but not part of the play. If we read the play with proper regard, we shall discern all this for ourselves. Actually we can discover it from the text; and Barrie's introductory remarks are to help those who read the words only, and do not see and hear with the eyes and ears of the actor and playwright.

Throughout the scene there are numerous directions to the actor and comments upon the characters. Read the actual dialogue carefully and you will realize that, actually, these parenthetical directions and comments are redundant for a reader who will try to understand and visualize the true implications of the language used by the various characters. They are to assist the reader who lacks a sense of the theatre, and those who will not pause to find the implications of dramatic dialogue. Dialogue represents only a portion of the actual dramatic conflict between characters; the other portion must be presented by the accompaniments of verbal expression that are seen in the theatre. These directions and descriptive passages in the printed text actually represent something of the work of the actor. They are Barrie's attempt at interpreting his dialogue for the reader.

All modern dramatists are fond of giving minute descriptions of their scenes and detailed instructions regarding interpretation. I strongly recommend you to expunge all these descriptions and instructions from your copy of a play. Having done so, read your play carefully, make your own description of the scene, and your own detailed notes regarding the acting accompaniments of the verbal expression. When you have done this there is no reason why you should not compare your notes with those of the dramatist. Study a scene of Barrie first to see how it is done, then do a scene yourself. This is a good way of cultivating a sense of the theatre, and power to visualize characters in action. Soon you will realize how much more interesting a play becomes when you read it with the intention of seeing and hearing it in your mind, than when you merely read on from speech to speech as if you were reading a novel or essay.

The dramatist reveals his characters and their story by the dialogue. Fortunately the plays of Shakespeare do not have these accompaniments to the dialogue, nor are the scenes given verbal description. Those who wish to read a Shakespearian play, or to act in one, must use their powers of imagination both with regard to its various settings and to verbal and character interpretation.

Let us then begin our study of interpretation by considering some of the characters in Shakespeare's plays. So much thought and time are devoted to the major characters in these that the great gallery of diverse secondary and minor characters is frequently passed over unnoticed. These minor characters are full of vitality, and so clearly drawn, with an

economy of language that is remarkable, that they must
always provide abundant interest for those who will but stay
to observe them.

Turn to Act I, Scene 2, of *Twelfth Night*. Let us find a way,
of interpreting the character of the Sea Captain. This is
the only scene in which this character appears. We all can
conjure up a picture of a sea captain; but, immediately, we
are aware that besides general characteristics each sea captain has his own particular character, and, in a play, his own
particular purpose. What can we discover about this one?

Carefully read the scene. Make yourself acquainted with
its contents, and also with what has gone before. Get a clear
mental picture of Viola, the Captain, and the sailors walking
along the coast, getting farther and farther away from the
wreck. Observe the relationship between Viola and the
Captain. Think of their respective attitudes towards their
present position. The one is fearful for the loss of her brother,
the other knows he has lost his ship. Viola is distressed and
weary, the Captain is thoughtful, but courageous and even
cheerful, in adversity. Notice the play with the word
"perchance" early in the scene, how it is echoed and re-
echoed.

Viola's—

> *Perchance* he is not drown'd

is echoed by the Captain's—

> It is *perchance* that you yourself were saved.

But the echo has just a shade of difference in tone and implication, which slowly penetrates Viola's sadness and is
re-echoed in her phrase—

> And so *perchance* may he be.

Then follows the Captain's long speech—an unusually
long speech for a sea captain. He must be very concerned
and have some very special purpose to be moved to such
an outburst of language. Study this speech beginning—

> True, madam; and to comfort you with *chance*,
> Assure yourself, after our ship did split,

Note its purpose. Surely it is to console Viola, to give her courage and to revive hope in her mind, and perhaps at the same time to produce in the minds of the audience some slight interest in the unnamed brother. Look at the speech again. Do not the words "Courage and hope" at the beginning of that parenthetical sentence seem to stand out beyond all else? And does not Viola immediately throw off her despair and lethargy? Does she not immediately rouse herself to action and assume the direction of her affairs? From this point she lives courageously and hopefully.

Rehearse this speech of the Captain. Speak it, keeping in mind its purpose. Will you not allow a sympathetic smile to play round your lips as you first address the lady? Will not your gruff voice assume some tenderness as you paint hopefully the picture of the young man's efforts to save himself? Will you not lengthen out, and linger on, the words "Courage and hope"?—and perhaps you will lift them ever so slightly in pitch, to give them emphasis and time to insinuate their intent upon the mind of Viola.

And what of gesture? Do you require any gesture to emphasize or direct the purpose of the speech? I think not. The intention of the language is remote from movement. It is never in any way emphatic, nor is it descriptive in its aim, which is rather that of insinuation. It is by its implication that its purpose is achieved. Gesture would very likely give undue emphasis to the drama of the sea and tend to lessen the effect of its true purport—namely, to focus attention upon Viola and revive within her hope and courage.

Turn now to Act IV, Scene 3, of *Twelfth Night* and study Sebastian's difficult soliloquy. Soliloquy is always difficult for the actor, but this one is rendered more so because the audience has no direct interest in Sebastian. All the more credit to the actor if he can compel the audience to be interested in him.

Search out Sebastian's mind from his language. We are aware of what has gone before. We know that Sebastian was filled with wonder at the words spoken to him by

Olivia, when she suddenly came between him and Sir Toby. Ever since that meeting and the subsequent episode which Shakespeare has kindly left us to imagine, Sebastian has lived in a whirl of excited expectancy and doubt. One moment he is in a state of the greatest ecstasy, the next he is overwhelmed by doubt and uncertainty. It is true that he possesses concrete evidence that this wonderful miracle did happen, but this only adds to his amazement and wonder. Olivia's beauty, her passionate avowal of love for him—a stranger—the sudden disappearance of Antonio, and now his betrothal to the beautiful and wealthy lady, completely overwhelm his senses. Surely there can be little wonder that Sebastian is not quite sure of his own state of mind.

This is the air, that is the glorious sun.

—is not this a definite reply to a doubt that would express itself, and does not the emphasis then naturally fall upon the repeated word "is," just as in the next line the emphasizing of "Feel't and see't" gives his mind the assurance it so badly needs, and carries him on to the pleasing conviction that "'tis not madness"? But at once he is brought down and back to his old thoughts by the appalling question—

Where is Antonio then?

In a real world a man does not disappear into thin air. Only in a world of fantasy can such things happen.

The answer—

I could not find him at the Elephant

is, however, eased by the consoling evidence that Antonio had been there, and so once again his mind is turned back towards the belief in his sanity. Again his words sweep on to the conclusion that he is mad, when suddenly and with almost horrifying realization his mind becomes aware of an alternative—

Or else the lady's mad;

The semicolon at the end of this phrase is indicative of the pause in his thoughts as he contemplates this possible sad catastrophe. But with gathering speed his mind once again argues the absurdity of this possibility, and settles down to the rational conclusion that—

> There's something in't
> That is deceivable.

And having reached this state of mind he is saved further worry and speculation by the coming of the lady herself. Can you not imagine the ecstasy of joy and relief that accompanies—

> But here the lady comes

and how the emotion holds him and swells into the simple but sincerely passionate utterance—

> I'll follow this good man, and go with you;
> And having sworn truth, ever will be true.

which leads on to the climax of the scene, Olivia's final speech? A lovely little scene this: an exquisite moment.

Go back over this speech and consider gesture. Does the soliloquy require any gesture? Undoubtedly Sebastian lifts his hand in order that he may feel and see the pearl upon his finger. Or if that pearl were on a pendant round his neck, then some similar gesture would be required. But I think, too, that the first line needs a gesture to assist the audience to follow the meaning of the words. There must be graceful movements of the hands and arms to indicate the air, and one hand moves upwards to indicate the sun. I like the pearl to be on a ring, then the concluding gesture completes the movements of the hands and brings them together as the ring is clasped in that definite assurance of the lady's existence.

The rest of the speech is ever-wavering debate, requiring emphasis only from the expression of the eyes and face, until the elation on seeing the lady inevitably causes the hands to be raised in eager greeting as Sebastian moves towards her.

In soliloquy the actor has to convey the impression that he is thinking aloud, and must not merely recite his words to the audience. In the modern theatre the soliloquy is rendered very difficult indeed. Yet its study and practice are a valuable exercise for the student, compelling concentration upon making speech, gesture, and movement the direct result of thought. IT MUST ALWAYS BE THE ACTOR'S AIM TO CREATE THE ILLUSION THAT HIS WORDS SPRING FROM HIS THOUGHTS.

To achieve this, the language must be searched until it surrenders the thoughts of the characters. So many students and amateurs regard the learning of the words as their most important task. They are happy when they have accomplished this. Actually the words they learn are but the symbols of that which really matters: the mind which they should reveal. This is one reason why an actor should be constantly asking himself: "Why have I to say this? What thought or feeling urges me to say this? What is the purpose of this speech?"

Not all thoughts, of course, are intense, nor are all feelings strong or deep. This is why so much of the dialogue of any play seems at first sight to be just so many words telling nothing more than a story. The actor, however, must realize that the most trivial phrase is the expression of thought, and that it does in some way and to some extent reveal the mind of the character. Even the "Good morning" of the maid to the mistress may be spoken to convey the degree of intimacy that exists between them.

The opening of Act I, Scene 3, of *The Merchant of Venice* is interesting—

> SHYLOCK: Three thousand ducats—well.
>
> BASSANIO: Ay, sir, for three months.
>
> SHYLOCK: For three months—well.
>
> BASSANIO: For the which as I told you, Antonio shall be bound.
>
> SHYLOCK: Antonio shall become bound—well.

What is the significance of the word "well" which concludes each of Shylock's speeches? It is only one word. But is its significance always the same? Are Shylock's thoughts always the same when he utters this word? What may be his thoughts as he says—

Antonio shall become bound?

And what may be the thoughts that follow the idea of Antonio being bonded? Can you speak the word "well" so that it has the illusion of being an exclamation arising from these thoughts? Try it. But surely it would not be proper to speak the other two "wells" in a similar manner. Then you must seek the thoughts of Shylock in order to know how to speak each of them.

It cannot be too often repeated that the actor's purpose is to reveal characters and their story to an audience. At the same time it may be appropriate to observe that essayists and literary scholars also achieve this. Charles Lamb, Coleridge, Professor Dowden, Dr. Dover Wilson, and many others have done much to clarify texts, and to reveal the characters of our great plays. They have done so by analysing, expounding, explaining, and criticizing. THE ACTOR MUST REVEAL BY CREATING AN ILLUSION THAT HE IS THE CHARACTER LIVING THROUGH THE EXPERIENCES SELECTED FOR HIM BY THE DRAMATIST.

The literary scholar sets down the character as he sees him, the actor shows the character himself, for others to see. We lack the power to see ourselves as others see us. Shylock did not know he was revengeful, malicious, or avaricious. He thought himself just, sincere, and thrifty. To you, Henry VIII may appear vulgar and cruel; to himself, he was natural and wise. You may dislike Henry; I am sure Henry liked himself very much indeed, and thought himself a fine specimen of a man.

AN ACTOR SHOULD NEVER IN HIS ACTING SHOW THAT HE IS CRITICIZING OR ASSESSING THE CHARACTER HE IS INTERPRETING.

Malvolio was a Puritan, a clever and capable steward, who was held in high respect by the Lady Olivia; he was

circumspect and decorous to a degree; he had the greatest
regard for right behaviour, and contempt for everything that
was common and vulgar. It is pitiable to watch actors trying
to make this character funny.

Some years ago, after a production of *Much Ado About
Nothing*, a young woman said to the young man who had
been playing the part of Claudio: "I could almost hate you.
You seemed to think it was noble to discard Hero." The
young man replied: "I don't know about the 'nobility,'
but I think Claudio was justified in what he did." That
young man was, of course, trying to think and speak as
Claudio, and he was right. The fact that the young woman
could "almost hate" him was clear vindication of his acting.

The scholar, the critic, and the audience observe a character in relation to their own ethical standards or those of the
play. An actor must interpret the standards of the character.
Iago was a villain. But Iago himself did not think in terms
of morality or good or evil. He was possessed by an insatiable
lust for power. He delighted in the ability to work mischief,
and in escaping from suspicion. His activity in hurting and
destroying was inexhaustible. Any means which enabled
him to attain his desires were justifiable. Success was his
ethical standard. The world that knew him thought him
honest, saw only a gay and skilful soldier whose friendship
was pleasant and desirable. He was sought after and his
advice was eagerly accepted by the many friends who gave
him their confidence. Iago took the greatest pains to appear
sincere, honest, and straightforward. His craft in achieving
this was his greatest asset. When the actor is made up to
look like a villain and is dressed in sinister black, he is robbed
of Iago's chief weapon of destruction, and makes all the
other characters of the play seem little more than a collection
of fools. Charles Lamb writes of Bensley's performance of this
part: "No spectator, from his action, could divine more of
his artifice than Othello was supposed to do. His confession
in soliloquy alone put you in possession of the mystery."

Barrie in his inimitable manner in *The Admirable Crichton*

draws a picture of an ignorant Cockney girl awakening to a
sense of the wonders around her. On the uninhabited island
upon which the unfortunate shipwrecked party finds itself,
little Tweeny discovers coco-nuts growing upon trees. To
Bill Crichton she expresses herself in these words:

I thought as how they grew in rows on tops of little sticks.

Here is a simple expression of ignorance. To speak it as
such would be a correct rendering of its meaning, but
scarcely a true interpretation of the spirit of the author, nor
the mind of Tweeny. Barrie has no intention here to cause
laughter by a display of ignorance from his beloved Tweeny,
but to show a simple mind awakening to the wonder and
mystery of a new-found world and a new truth. The spirit
of the Renaissance is awakening in the mind of Tweeny.

Visualize the picture made by Crichton and Tweeny,
hear in your mind their voices as they talk of Tweeny's
discovery of the coco-nuts. Her eyes are aglow with *wonder*
as she kneels by the side of Crichton; in humbleness she
bows her head as she senses her own depth of ignorance;
in eagerness her spirit reaches out to this new sense of beauty
and knowledge that she finds for the first time.

Here in brief is the actor's task and his joy. No small task
this. It will not be easy to communicate to an audience the
mind of Tweeny, but when this romantic implication is
interpreted by carefully selected tones, by appropriate
emphasis and intensity, and by delicate gesture and facial
expression, the actress and her audience will be very close
to the spirit of Barrie.

Here is the task of the actor. First, to search for the
character, the mental outlook, and the spirit to be discovered from the language; then to find a way to communicate these to an audience. The dramatist communicates
by language. The words must be studied and searched until
they reveal all that is to be known of the character and his
story. It is not enough to understand the meaning of the
words, for these may be but the symbols of something far

more important. They may be the significant signs of a
great emotion or idea. The actor must appreciate the mind
of the character he is playing, he must possess the thoughts
and the feelings which have given birth to the words.

Professor Higgins is a bully, he is a master of phonetics,
he is eccentric, and has mannerisms and habits that are
offensive. The language he uses indicates all this. But he
is something more than this. Were these his only qualities,
he would be unbearable. One could not endure his conceit,
his overpowering intolerance, and his cruelty. Higgins,
from a normal point of view, is the worst teacher that ever
taught; from the same point of view he is entirely obnoxious
as a human being. He is, however, saved by his genius.
He is an artist whose vision, knowledge, and ability raise
him above and beyond normal standards. His physical
attributes, his social misdemeanours, his conceit, and his
bullying are trifles when set against the greatness of the
idea which inspires his thought and intellectual activity.
Behaviour, which is the chief possession of the normal man,
is but the humorous eccentricity of the great artist.

The actor playing the part of Higgins cannot fail to convey the lesser attributes of this character. He has but to
speak the words as Shaw has written them to achieve this.
But if he does only this he has merely interpreted a bully, a
bad teacher, and an insufferable bore: a man who should
have been horse-whipped. To interpret the real Professor
Higgins the actor must reveal the mind of a great artist
possessed of a vital purpose, a spark of divine fire. He is a
visionary, a poet, a reformer, and in one respect a great
teacher. If the actor concentrates his interpretation upon
the real Professor, the audience will see those other qualities
in their true and proper relationship to the man. Only so
are they truly humorous.

Constantly one is being asked: "Should an actor feel the
emotion of the character he is interpreting?" The question
has been argued many times. Some actors will tell you that
they always feel the emotions of their prototype; others

will deny the necessity of doing so. Some actresses have
wept real tears in their performances, others could not,
even though they would. For many reasons, reminiscence
helps us but little towards a solution. And perhaps it does
not matter either way. Is it not reasonable to believe that
actors approach their task and succeed in their presentation
by travelling along different routes? There may be as many
roads to interpretation as there are to Rome.

I do not know how one feels when drunk. Perhaps no one
does, though many may be painfully conscious of the feelings
of a "hang-over." But I do know something of the effects
of alcohol, and I have clear mental images of the outward
signs of being drunk. I am also aware that some of the
attributes of those suffering from a surfeit of alcoholic liquor
would not assist in an interpretation of Borachio, Sir Andrew
Aguecheek, or even of Sir Toby Belch. The mere mention
of these names surely also suggests that even the doubtful
quality of being drunk is a personal thing. These three *do*
get drunk, but ever so differently. And their tasks while
drunk are also different. Does not this lead us to realize
that for interpretation an actor *selects* from the memories
and mental images of past experiences, and shapes from these
a new experience for others to behold? THUS DOES THE
ACTOR CREATE.

One thing seems to be certain: an actor cannot interpret
that which is entirely outside his experience, or beyond
his capacity of appreciation. In *Milestones* a character
describes the launching of the first iron ship. For him, and
for all who saw this great event and achievement, it was as
thrilling as any miracle could be. The seemingly impossible
had been accomplished. In each scene of this play a fresh
"miracle" stirs the imagination and arouses the wonder of
those capable of being thrilled. In these days, when wonders
follow upon wonders with the rapidity of thought, it becomes
ever more difficult to be thrilled. The youth of to-day tends
to become blasé and to accept every new achievement as
a matter of course. The actor, and those who wish to act,

must retain and cultivate the power of feeling. They must retain their capacity for being thrilled, they must keep themselves alive and receptive. The actor must be able to feel, or at least to simulate feeling, in order that he may be able to make others feel and understand.

SUMMARY

1. Drama is concerned with characters.
2. The dramatist reveals his characters and their story by the dialogue.
3. The Sea Captain in *Twelfth Night*.
4. Sebastian's soliloquy.
5. It must always be the actor's aim to create the illusion that his words spring from his thoughts.
6. The actor must reveal by creating an illusion that he is the character living through the experiences selected for him by the dramatist.
7. An actor should never in his acting show that he is criticizing or assessing the character he is interpreting.
8. An actor must interpret the moral and ethical standards of the character himself.
9. The character of Tweeny in *The Admirable Crichton*.
10. The actor's task is first to search for the character, the mental outlook, and the spirit to be discovered from the language, then to find a way to communicate these to an audience.
11. The character of Professor Higgins in *Pygmalion*.
12. Should an actor feel the emotion of the character he is interpreting?
13. An actor creates by selecting from the memories and mental images of past experiences, and shaping from these a new experience for others to behold.
14. An actor must be able to feel, or at least to simulate feeling, in order that he may be able to make others feel and understand.

EXERCISES ON CHAPTER VII

1. *Antigone*, by Sophocles. (Elsie Fogerty's Edition.) Messenger's speech in the Exodus, beginning—
> Dear lady, I will tell of what I saw.

What do we know of the personality of the messenger? Very little, except that he is straightforward and blunt of speech. What is the purpose of this narrative, and how will you achieve the task of communicating it to the audience? Mark passages spoken directly to the Queen and those that are addressed to the Chorus. Note changes in pace, underline words and phrases that must be stressed to bring out a clear picture of the events narrated. What is the climax of the speech?

2. *The Merchant of Venice:* Act I, Scene 3.

Study this scene, writing in stage directions, parenthetical directions, and comments, as a modern dramatist might do. Is it necessary to describe the place in which this scene takes place? Write notes of the acting accompaniments of verbal expression. Differentiate the attitudes of Bassanio and Antonio towards Shylock.

3. *Twelfth Night:* Act III, Scene 4. Antonio's speeches beginning—

I must obey. This comes with seeking you.

Compare the personality of this Sea Captain with the one already met in Act I, Scene 2.

What is the dramatic purpose of Antonio in this scene?

4. *Richard III:* Act I, Scene 1. The Duke of Gloucester's opening soliloquy—

Now is the winter of our discontent
Made glorious summer by this sun of York.

Note the dual purpose of this soliloquy. It establishes the personality and character of Richard, and at the same time it informs the audience regarding certain historical details and Gloucester's personal aims. This speech makes an interesting study. Note the irony which is a distinguishing feature of this egocentric character.

Intensity of stress to emphasize the contrasting words and phrases will be the chief medium of interpretation. Probably there will be little movement and scarcely any gesture.

5. Compare this soliloquy with those of Edmund in Act I, Scene 2, of *King Lear*, and Iago in Act II, Scene 1, of *Othello*.

6. *Antony and Cleopatra:* Act IV, Scene 6. The final soliloquy of Enobarbus.

Search the language here and that which precedes it for the thoughts and emotions of Enobarbus. Pathos and nobility of soul blend in the final words and exit.

7. *The Rivals:* Act III, Scene 2. Faulkland's soliloquy beginning—

They told me Julia would return directly; I wonder she is not yet come!

A very difficult speech. Study it closely and search for the ever-wavering thoughts of this jealously devoted lover. Phrasing and stress are of the utmost importance.

8. *The School for Scandal.*

Consider the three characters: Sir Peter Teazle, Joseph Surface, and Charles Surface.

What characteristics of each of these men would you try to communicate to your audience?

9. *The School for Scandal:* Act I, Scene 2. Sir Peter Teazle's soliloquy—

When an old bachelor marries a young wife, what is he to expect?

Study this speech and try to convey something of the personality of Sir Peter while giving the sense of the thoughts which give rise to the language.

10. *The School for Scandal:* Act IV, Scene 1. Charles Surface's speech beginning—

Aye, aye, these are done in the true spirit of portrait painting.

This is good comedy and at the same time the language surrenders the personality of the gay Charles.

11. *The School for Scandal:* Act I, Scene 1. Joseph Surface's speech beginning—

True, madam; notwithstanding his vices one can't help feeling for him.

Speak this speech smoothly and with such sincerity that even your worst enemy would believe you honest.

12. *Call it a Day,* by Dodie Smith. Act II, Scene 1.

Consider the characters of the artist's wife and Catherine. How will you sit and look to suggest the attitude of Catherine to the artist? How will you act to suggest the attitude of the wife to Catherine?

13. *The Lady with a Lamp,* by Reginald Berkeley: Act II, Scene 4.

What does this scene reveal of the character of Florence Nightingale? Study especially the dialogue from the entrance of Tremayne on the stretcher, and search for the thoughts from which the language springs.

14. *Berkeley Square,* by John Balderston: Act 2. Kate's speech beginning—

Oh, I can't do that. How smugly you say it!

Read the preceding dialogue to understand the feelings of Kate at this moment. Try to express the great fear from which she suffers, and the contempt she has for this strange man who has come to marry her.

15. *Berkeley Square:* Act III, Scene 1. Helen's speech beginning—

What life is this for you?

Try to suggest the simple sincerity of this speech. Tone and emphasis of selected words.

16. *The Kingdom of God,* by Sierra: Act I. The opening dialogue between the two old men, Gabriel and Trajano.

Visualize these two old men. Think of them as physical beings. Sit and walk as they do. Practise their stage business. Speak the language to suggest their personalities and to convey the story. This makes an interesting study of two excellent old men characters.

17. *Will Shakespeare,* by Clemence Dane: Act IV. Elizabeth's speech beginning—

I thought so, too,
When I was young

down to—

. . . to have her story

Do not these words reveal something of the bitterness and suffering of this great English queen? Speak this speech over and over again until you can convey the full implications of the language.

18. *Bird in Hand,* by John Drinkwater: Act 1. Mr. Blanquet's speech beginning—

I told you so. But it's true.

Blanquet is a Cockney. We have to consider his dialect. Charming comedy, this.

Compare this speech with Doolittle's, beginning—

Don't say that, Governor. Don't look at it that way.

in Act II of *Pygmalion.*

Dialect, gesture, and deportment will demand great attention.

CHAPTER VIII

ENTRANCES

THE experienced actor realizes how important entrances are, both for his individual success and for the appropriate interpretation of the play. The less experienced, unfortunately, often leave their entrances to chance, or rehearse them so indifferently that regrettable mishaps result.

Immediately an actor comes into view of the audience he is concerned with the action of the play. Entrances necessarily arouse a fresh interest. It is of vital importance that this interest shall carry forward the movement of the scene and not interrupt its development by any extraneous or untoward accident or incident.

To enter the stage effectively, at any time and in any circumstances, it is necessary for an actor to acquire skill in the mechanics of movement. He must be able to walk on the stage, to run, to amble, to walk downstairs, to carry trays and parcels, to turn easily, and so on. Exercises in such mechanical tasks may be a little irksome, and many actors will consider the practice unnecessary; but facility in walking to a given place on the stage, in turning at will, in putting something down or picking something up, in a manner that indicates ease and certainty, gives a "finish" to stage work that is most pleasing and effective. On the other hand, when these mechanical tasks are performed clumsily and self-consciously they distract attention from the main interest of a scene and offend the discriminating.

Because the camera is most sensitive to factual realities, and the "movies" are properly concerned with movement, the cinema very naturally provides an enormous variety of excellent examples of how to walk into a room, how to walk downstairs, how to run into a room or into an open space.

The mechanics of stage work are admirably demonstrated by the cinema stars. They are proud of their skill in these details. It is common for film producers to show a "close-up" of a door being opened quietly and a man sidling through the doorway. They revel in letting the audience see a great star running quickly down a long stairway, or walking with ever-increasing speed until he is suddenly pulled up by some material or imaginary obstacle. For the "movies" these mechanical skills represent much that is highest in the art of the cinema. Such skill may be of no outstanding merit on the stage; nevertheless, aspiring actors can learn much both from the methods of screen artists and from their use of these mechanical aids to interpretation and technical efficiency. Such skill may not achieve interpretation, but its lack will render interpretation difficult, if not impossible.

You have learned that everything you do on the stage must have a purpose. YOU MUST HAVE A PURPOSE FOR YOUR ENTRANCE. Your purpose and method of entering will be modified by several considerations that may be stated simply as follows—

(*a*) Your character.

(*b*) The previous circumstances—not always stated by the author.

(*c*) The immediate purpose laid down by the author.

Try this little sketch—

The curtain goes up on an empty drawing-room. You are a servant. You enter the stage to bring in some letters. The curtain falls.

In this exercise some indication is given of your character —you are a servant. The previous circumstances are not indicated. You may be aware that the room is empty. On the other hand, you may not know this until after you have entered. It must be obvious that this factor will considerably affect the manner in which you, being a servant, will enter the room. Your immediate purpose is to deliver letters, and your method of doing so will be influenced by your previous knowledge of those likely to be occupying the room, and also by the "quality" of the people you are serving.

Here is another exercise—

The curtain goes up on an empty room. It is your room, and you enter with a heavy parcel. It is a hot day in August and you have come some distance. The curtain comes down.

Note: (*a*) Character—For the purpose of this exercise you are given freedom with regard to your individual character.

(*b*) Previous circumstances—It is a room with which you are familiar. It is a hot day and you have come some distance.

All these factors will affect your method of entering, and you have to try to interpret all these conditions.

Compare this exercise with the entrance of Freddy Eynesford Hill in Act I of *Pygmalion*.

In both these exercises there is a condition not yet mentioned. To enter a room it is generally necessary to pass through a doorway. To many beginners doors are troublesome obstacles. Rehearsals usually take place in a space marked out on the floor of a room. Doors are not used; frequently they are not even considered until the dress rehearsal. But the doors must be taken into account or the results may be disastrous.

This may seem to be little more than an unimportant trifle, but when a play is being rehearsed for performance there is frequently insufficient time for the proper rehearsal of such details. For this reason it is necessary for all who wish to take part in the performance of plays to acquire skill in these simple technical details. By so doing, they make it possible for rehearsal time to be devoted to the problems rightly belonging to it.

By practice you can acquire the habit of opening a door, entering a room, and closing a door. In rehearsing this simple activity, you must know whether your door will open on to the stage or away from it. You must cultivate the habit of turning a handle, moving the door either away from you or towards you, and, after passing through, closing it after you. This ability to enter through a doorway on to the stage must be regarded as an elementary skill which all actors should acquire.

Frequently a stage is enclosed by curtains and not by fixtures. This type of boundary is sometimes given as an excuse for not bothering to rehearse or to acquire skill in making an entrance. But, if you have realized the fact that immediately you are in view of the audience you are concerned with the action of the play, you will have to grant that entrances through curtains need to be made with just as much care as when made through a realistic doorway. You must acquire skill in opening and closing curtains or the displaced and untidy background will have a very disturbing effect upon the minds of the audience.

Scenes, however, are not always set in the confined space of a room. Let us rehearse one set in an open space—

The curtain goes up on part of a wood. You and a friend enter. You have come some distance and are delighted to find shelter in the wood. The curtain comes down.

What are the conditions in this exercise?

(*a*) Again, freedom is given with regard to the characters, except that they are friends.

(*b*) Previous circumstances—they have come some distance and we may presume that they are tired from their exertions. There is room for imagination with regard to some points. The exercise does not say if the characters are laden, nor does it indicate whether it is hot or raining.

(*c*) Immediate condition—delight at finding shelter.

This exercise might well be followed by preparing openings of scenes having similar conditions. A scene which at once comes to mind is *Twelfth Night*, Act I, Scene 2. Here Viola and the Sea Captain enter on the sea coast of Illyria, in circumstances not unlike those in the exercise given above.

In rehearsing this scene, it is important to visualize the characters, the circumstances which have brought them to this coast, and the immediate purpose of the scene.

Rehearse a number of openings of scenes in which one or two characters enter. Have a clearly defined purpose when making your entrances, so that you may immediately establish your character, indicate the previous circumstances, and the immediate purpose.

Here is another exercise for a group of actors—

The curtain goes up on two characters sitting in a room. As they talk they are interrupted by the entrance of a third character. The curtain comes down.

In every play you will find situations similar to the one given here. Yet, almost inevitably, the performance will produce some confusion unless careful thought and planning are given to it. Confusion will be caused because no common purpose has been stated, and because no relationship of any kind has been expressed between the characters, and also because no time has been fixed for the entrance of the third party, and for several other reasons which may not be obvious at the moment.

Actors generally are tempted to regard their work in isolation, but such a scene as this may be successfully achieved only when all concerned have a common purpose; when each actor fully understands the relationships existing between them all, and when all know the exact moment when the third character will enter.

Let us add some conditions—

The curtain goes up. Two characters are conversing in a friendly manner. They are expecting a mutual friend. They hear him coming. He knocks and enters. There are mutual greetings. The curtain comes down.

The added conditions will help the actors considerably, but still there is much to determine before a satisfactory entrance can be completed. Were this scene to take place in real life, the order and method of greeting would perhaps not matter, but on the stage, when everything done must have an immediate purpose and lead naturally to that which follows, it will be of importance to know the exact positions those on the stage will occupy when the third character enters, to determine the order in which the characters shall greet each other, and the exact positions of each character when the greetings are made, and the positions they assume immediately subsequent to the greetings. It will be worth while to rehearse this exercise carefully because so many entrances in actual plays are similar in nature and carry with them similar problems.

The opening of *Twelfth Night*, Act I, Scene 3, is very similar to this exercise. In this scene the entrance of Sir Andrew Aguecheek is of considerable interest. Unlike modern authors, Shakespeare provides us with few stage directions. This is really fortunate, for their absence compels all concerned to study the text of the play with due and proper care.

The actor playing the part of Sir Andrew must study the play in order to appreciate his character; he will get no other help from Shakespeare. From a study of this scene, he will discover that Sir Andrew has determined that his mission in Illyria is doomed to failure, and that his purpose in this scene is to acquaint Sir Toby with his decision to leave for home.

From the text he will further note that while Sir Toby and Sir Andrew are friends, Sir Andrew and Maria have not previously met. He will also realize that Sir Andrew expected to find Sir Toby, but that he was unaware of the presence of Maria. Sir Andrew's natural impetuosity, and his eagerness to let his friend know of his sudden determination to go home, cause him to burst in upon Sir Toby; but the presence of the strange serving woman checks him, and he lamely exclaims, "How now, Sir Toby Belch!", and he awkwardly and timidly accepts a formal introduction to Maria.

For this entrance of Sir Andrew to be achieved with any

success not only is it necessary for Sir Andrew to understand his character and purpose, but it is also of equal importance that Sir Toby and Maria shall be in appropriate positions on the stage, so that the sudden check to Sir Andrew's impetuosity and his subsequent introduction may appear natural and spontaneous. It is the business of the producer to establish these positions; it is the duty of those playing Sir Toby and Maria to see that they are in those positions.

The entrance of a character ought never to be regarded in isolation, but should be considered as an action in which all those on the stage play their part. Team work in the matter of entrances is of vital significance in the interpretation of a play. A study of the entrances of the various characters in *Pygmalion*, Act III, should prove of considerable interest, and will illustrate the importance of realizing that, while it may be true that one character comes on to the stage at a given moment, the actual entrance is the concern of every character on the stage at that time.

The first entrance in this scene from *Pygmalion* is made by Professor Higgins. On the stage, sitting at a writing desk, diagonally opposite the door, is Mrs. Higgins, Henry's mother. The door is opened violently; and Higgins enters with his hat on. Mrs. Higgins speaks, and, as Henry stoops down to kiss her, she removes his hat and hands it to him, as he exclaims, "Oh bother!" and throws the hat down on the table. The character entering is an eccentric professor; he has been hurrying in order that he may talk with his mother before her usual guests arrive; he opens the door violently and hurries across the room to greet her.

Practise first the entrance through the doorway. Open the door violently, and close it before passing quickly across the room. If, in your hurry, you allow the door to slam behind you, you will most probably render Mrs. Higgins's speech inaudible, and if you do not close the door after you, you will cause trouble for the subsequent part of the scene. You must close the door after you with as quick an action as possible, and then hurry across the room to your waiting mother.

You must arrive at the place where she is sitting so that you can bend over to kiss her just as she is finishing her speech. She should have removed your hat at the exact moment that she concludes her speech. She removes the hat and hands it to you in one movement, as you reply "Oh bother!"

Rehearse this entrance until you are successful in timing the movements with the speech, so that there is no break in the action from the opening of the door to the throwing down of the hat on the table. It is an interesting entrance, both from the point of view of the actual swift movements of Higgins, and because of the need for timing these movements with the dialogue.

The need for accurate timing in making an entrance is again clearly illustrated when the maid enters to announce Mrs. and Miss Eynesford Hill. Higgins is explaining to his mother how his work with Eliza has progressed, when they are interrupted by the parlour-maid announcing the guests. In making this entrance the maid has to open the door, enter, and make the announcement as Higgins says the word "where——."

The entrance must be unhurried, and the announcement made immediately the girl is on the stage. The situation is stupid if she has to wait on the stage until she hears her cue, and, of course, for her to keep Higgins and his mother waiting for the announcement is even more silly. Practise this entrance, and as many similar ones as you like, until you find it a simple matter to time an entrance correctly. It is of great importance to develop a sense of "timing."

The entrance of Mrs. Eynesford Hill and her daughter, Clara, is interesting because of the difference between these two characters and their attitudes towards the professor. Get your copy of *Pygmalion* and rehearse from the entrance of these two characters down to the moment when they are finally seated. This little episode makes a delightful study in entering, moving, and timing.

When the maid announced them, Henry was sitting on an ottoman in the centre of the stage, talking to his mother, who was seated at her desk. The interruption causes both to rise—Henry angrily, Mrs. Higgins eager to greet her visitors.

As the two Eynesford Hills move across the room to shake hands with Mrs. Higgins, Henry grabs his hat from the table and tries to steal out of the room.

Just as he reaches the door, his mother introduces him to Mrs. Eynesford Hill. This movement is intricate, but, when done with apparent spontaneity, delightfully funny.

To obtain the effect of spontaneity the entrance and subsequent dialogue must be achieved with absolute mechanical accuracy. Actually, the movements and the speech must be controlled and timed with just as much care as are the steps of a dance. This is a paradox that all must learn: controlled and accurately timed movement and speech will suggest ease, sincerity, and spontaneity. Uncontrolled and badly-timed movement and speech will convey a sense of artificiality, uneasiness, and insincerity.

The actual entrance of these two ladies is not completed until they are safely seated. During the time it takes, both are able to give clear indications of their separate characters, the dialogue establishes the part they have already played, and all on the stage are intimately concerned with the actual entrance.

Whenever a character comes on the stage, fresh interest is aroused. Sometimes it happens that the character is of such importance that the play's action is for the moment arrested. Everybody waits for this character to give re-direction to the development of the scene. Such a moment is the entrance of Portia in the Trial Scene of *The Merchant of Venice*; another is the first entrance of Lob in *Dear Brutus*.

At such moments every one on the stage has to focus attention upon the entering figure. At the same time they must indicate their own individual reactions to the new arrival. In effecting this they must take care that nothing they do shall distract the attention of the audience from the principal character. The audience must be directly conscious of the new character coming upon the scene, but in the margin of their consciousness they must also be aware of the effect this character makes upon those already on the stage.

These moments are very important and require the most careful rehearsal. They are moments that should in performance be stressed in order that their significance may be rightly appreciated and remembered.

The entrance of Lob is particularly interesting. The audience have heard about this queer, very old man, and are eager to meet him. The way has been prepared by the dialogue, and especially by Matey. It is a slow entrance, for Lob is so very old. He passes across the room, noticing everybody, but never saying a word. The silence has to be made interesting, and, indeed, informative, for only so will the audience's attention be held during that long period of time.

Perhaps a clue as to what really takes place during this entrance may be found when it is realized that only one person on the stage actually likes Lob. Mrs. Coade likes him; is indeed very fond of him. The others fear, distrust, or definitely dislike him. At the same time it should be noted that Lob is very fond of Mrs. Coade. He almost hates Mrs. Dearth, and is devilishly amused at Joanna. Perhaps these thoughts can be communicated by Lob and those others on the stage as he walks across the room.

Processional entrances also need careful rehearsal. These actually make excellent exercises in walking on the stage, and in precision of movement.

Consider the entrance of Lear, with his daughters and the rest of his court, in Act I of *King Lear*. Everything done must possess dignity and order. The entrance must be achieved without undue loss of time, and characters must get into their right positions without fuss or conufsion. Such entrances must be organized as a massed drill would be organized, yet they must be distinguished from a march of a troop of soldiers. While they enter as a unit, the individual characters must be allowed to preserve their individuality. Their entrance must not be treated as a march, nor may the characters have the licence of a crowd.

A specialized form of processional entrance may be seen towards the end of Act I of *Dear Brutus*.

Lob leads his guests on to the stage in readiness for their proposed walk to search for Lob's Wood. The guests actually crowd on to the stage. Such a direction sounds very simple, but in practice it is most difficult. This is not just a crowd of people, but a collection of individuals each of whom has to play a definite part in the rest of the scene. This fact renders necessary the allotment to each character of a special order of entrance and a special place to go to on the stage.

Again, we find it necessary to organize the entrance as a drill. Only so can order be maintained and a seeming spontaneity created. This entrance can be organized only when we are aware of the purpose each character has to fulfil during the part of the scene which immediately follows. The entrance can be made to appear natural and spontaneous only when each individual carries out his part accurately and precisely.

SUMMARY

1. **Immediately an actor comes into view of the audience he becomes concerned with the action of the play.**
2. **An actor must acquire skill in the mechanics of movement.**
3. **You must have a purpose for your entrance.**
4. **Entrances are modified by character, previous circumstances, and the immediate purpose.**
5. **The importance of doors.**
6. **The entrance of a character ought never to be regarded in isolation, but should be considered as a concerted action in which all those on the stage play their part.**
7. **"Timing" is an essential condition of making an entrance.**
8. **Controlled and accurately-timed movement and speech will suggest ease, sincerity, and spontaneity; uncontrolled and badly timed, they will convey a sense of artificiality.**
9. **Whenever a character comes on the stage, fresh interest is aroused.**
10. **Processional entrances.**

EXERCISES ON CHAPTER VIII

1. *Henry V:* Act III, Scene 2. Entrance of Fluellen and Gower.

In this scene Fluellen must enter first. Both are walking rapidly, and speak with speed, especially Fluellen.

2. *Twelfth Night:* Act II, Scene 1. Entrance of Antonio and Sebastian.

These two characters are walking along together. Entrances of this kind are difficult unless the actors think of the previous circumstances.

3. *Julius Caesar:* Act III, Scene 1. Opening of scene.

Requires crowd control and the organizing of a processional entrance.

4. *The Merchant of Venice:* Act IV, Scene 1. Entrance of the Duke of Venice.

5. *Twelfth Night:* Act II, Scene 3. Entrance of Sir Toby and Sir Andrew.

Both characters have had more than enough to drink. This is an entrance which demands attention to character and purpose.

6. *Twelfth Night:* Act V. Entrance of Sebastian.

Note the effect of this entrance upon all on the stage. It is a thrilling moment for each character, especially for Viola, Olivia, Orsino, and Antonio.

7. *Quality Street,* by J. M. Barrie: Act I. Entrance of Patty with tea.

8. *Berkeley Square,* by John Balderston: Act I, Scene 2. Entrance of Mrs. Barwick with tea-tray.

9. *Berkeley Square:* Act I, Scene 3. Entrance of Peter at beginning of scene.

Same scene—first entrance of Lady Anne.

10. *Berkeley Square:* Act II. Entrance of the Duke of Cumberland.

This is an extremely difficult entrance to control. All on the stage take important parts in this particular entrance, and their acting must be of the most formal character.

11. *Will Shakespeare,* by Clemence Dane: Act II—towards end of the scene. Entrance of Mary, after she has played the part of Juliet.

12. *The Kingdom of God,* by Sierra: Act III. Entrance of Juan De Dios, the bull-fighter.

13. *Escape,* by John Galsworthy: Part I, Episode 3. Entrance of Matt from behind the curtain; also the entrance of Lady from the bathroom.

14. *Secrets,* by Rudolf Besier: Act II. Shack scene. Entrance of Bob—
Boss, quick—they're on us—.

15. *Women at War.* One-act play by Edward Percy.

In this little piece there are many interesting entrances which depend for their effect on timing and by-play of actresses on the stage.

16. *Elizabeth Refuses,* by Margaret Macnamara. The first entrance of Mr. Collins with Mrs. Bennett.

17. *Riders to the Sea,* by J. M. Synge.

Rehearse from Nora's speech—

Did you hear that, Cathleen? Did you hear a noise in the north-east?

down to Maurya's speech—

They're all gone now, and there isn't anything more the sea can do to me.

The entrances of the old women, the two young women, and the men carrying in the body of Bartley are of considerable dramatic importance.

18. *The Theatre,* by Rubenstein.

This one-act play provides a number of most interesting entrances, rehearsal of which will give much valuable experience.

19. *Reunion,* by W. St. John Tayleur.

The entrance of "The Figure" presents an unusual and most interesting problem. The actual entrance of "The Figure" is slow, quiet and dignified. Its effect must arrest the attention of those on the stage and the audience. It must provide a "mystery." It is an important climacteric and its effect upon each of those already on the stage must be studied.

20. *Where the Cross is Made,* by Eugene O'Neill.

The entrance of the Mate, the Bo'sun, and the Harpooner of the Schooner *Mary Allen* carrying the treasure is a moment of intense drama, especially in its effect upon the characters already on the stage. It is one that demands care from the producer and studied individual acting from members of the cast. It also presents an interesting opportunity for lighting.

CHAPTER IX

Play Production: Stage and Interpretation

MODERN theorists tell us that a play consists of all that is seen and heard in a theatre. They argue that scenery, lighting, properties, and costume are as much a part of it as are the characters and their dialogue. This is a fascinating aesthetic theory, supported mainly by designers and electricians, but receiving little confirmation from dramatists. Clearly, great dramatists such as Aeschylus, Sophocles, Euripides, Shakespeare, Sheridan, and, in our own time, Barrie, Shaw, Yeats, Masefield, and Galsworthy, had not this conception of a play when they were writing their great dramas. Perhaps it is more applicable to a drama which has yet to be born and is still in process of visualization.

For the dramatist a play is concerned with characters and their story as revealed to an audience by actors. The only essentials for dramatic presentation are a play, an acting space, an auditorium, and actors. No one would deny the value of lighting or stage decoration, but these should never be more than the servants of the actor to assist him in his task of interpretation. Many modern Shakespearian productions have had wonderful lighting effects and original and beautiful stage constructions, but it is doubtful whether these revealed or clarified any part of the text or character.

The modern developments in the theatre are indeed wonderful and beautiful in themselves, but frequently their beauty is so astonishing and attractive that interest is deflected from the human conflict with which the play is rightly concerned. The mind becomes absorbed by the symbolism of a shaft of light, or bewildered by the psychological significance of mechanical construction, while the words and the actors are lost in a confusion of colour, architecture, and light.

In the great Greek and Shakespearian periods, plays were

presented before a formal background which was always
the same for any and every play, and which was well known
to the audience. The familiarity with this formal setting
resulted in the actor and the dialogue being of supreme
interest. The actual acting space was a place on which a
play was performed; it was not a part of the play. It is
true that conditions within the theatre have changed since
those times, and these necessarily have brought about a
change in method of production, but the essential conditions
of drama have not changed. Language and character are
still the essentials of a play, human conflict is still the
concern of the dramatist, and the actor must still be the
supreme artist on the stage. His background should be of
interest through him and not for its own sake.

A few years ago some amateurs performed *Twelfth Night*
in a school hall, on a small stage which was enclosed by
curtains of a neutral colour. For the garden scene a simple
conventional hedge was the sole property. This piece of
"scenery" looked nothing like a hedge, but both the actors
and the audience tacitly agreed that "it was a hedge." It
served to indicate the garden, and also to hide Sir Toby
Belch, Sir Andrew Aguecheek, and Fabian, while Malvolio
read the letter purporting to come from the Lady Olivia.
Everybody who saw the scene agreed that it was a great
success.

Some time later these amateurs performed the same play
on a large stage, on which was set a beautiful garden scene,
with realistic trees, hedges, and flowers against a magnificent
cyclorama which gave a sense of great spaciousness. This
wonderful representation of a factual garden thrilled everybody—everybody, that is, except the unfortunate actors.
They were helpless. Their by-play, effective before, was
useless.

A friend who saw both performances could not understand
why this scene, which had been such a success in the school
hall, should be so tame on this wonderfully decorated and
"sunlit" stage. The truth was that in the performance in the

school hall interest was focused upon the players and the action of the play, while in the theatre the brilliant lighting and the magnificence of the realistic setting absorbed interest and hindered the actors in their important task of interpretation. For the performance in the school hall the stage was set to assist the actors—it was consciously planned in relation to their work. In the theatre, the stage manager had interpreted his idea of a garden, and the actors were invited to perform in it as they might be in any garden into which they had been accidentally flung. This factual garden had no relation at all with the planned action of the scenes to be enacted in it. It was of the greatest interest for its own sake, it was startlingly beautiful, but it had been conceived without reference to the actors and their parts.

Actually, although a great part of this play takes place in a garden, it is not about the garden. The play is concerned with certain selected characters and their doings over a chosen period of time. The garden is really of no significance in the play. So lively are the characters and so beautiful is the language that this play could most effectively be rendered on a curtained stage with screens appropriately disposed, as, indeed, it has been in the National Theatre in Prague.

Few scenes demand factual representation of background, yet it has become a common practice for stages to be set about with painted canvas. On the amateur stage these painted sets are rarely satisfactory. Usually the doors do not fit and the walls wobble. No one is deceived into thinking them anything but what they are—canvas and paint. They rarely assist the actor; often they hinder him. The desire for painted scenery is usually little more than an unreasonable attempt to imitate the professional theatre, and on the amateur stage the result is frequently a poor makeshift for something that can be achieved only by a considerable expenditure of money and labour.

I am surprised that screens are not more frequently used as background for acting spaces. They are flexible. They can be placed in any desired position. They can be draped or covered to create practically any desired effect. With them it is possible to arrange for entrances at any point, and the size and shape of the acting space can be controlled with ease. This is of considerable importance, because some scenes play more effectively in small spaces, while others play to advantage on a stage not rectangular in shape. By careful and imaginative disposition considerable variety can be suggested for the various scenes of a play, which will aid its appreciation by an audience. It is wrong, I believe, to regard screens merely as a makeshift for something better. They are makeshifts only when they are arranged round an acting space like so many scenic "flats," as if they were apologizing for not being the actual walls of a room. Let them appear as screens against which the scene is played and they can be most pleasing and effective.

Audiences are generally quite willing to join in a game of "let's pretend," but they will not accept as reality that which is obviously a fake. The essence of drama is illusion, and the illusion of a kitchen, drawing-room, or bedroom is more readily created by an appropriate piece of furniture than it is by the most elaborately painted "walls."

A stage that is enclosed by curtains of neutral colour, hung on runners, and provided with a traverse curtain for scenes requiring less space than the full stage, will provide an acting space suitable for almost any play. The curtains make a pleasing and practicable setting, entrances are easily arranged, and there is no arduous changing of "sets" between the scenes. The curtain is suitable for any scene except the few that demand special factual presentation for their interpretation. It would be difficult, of course, to create an illusion of John Carlton's shack, in Act II o *Secrets*, being attacked and destroyed. For such a scene some sort of structure must be erected, since the action of the play is directly concerned with the building. In this scene the realism of the setting is almost as important as that of the drama. Emotional interest is intensified by the falling oil-lamp and the battering in of a section of the wall. But such scenes are rare. The majority of scenes are not directly related to, or dependent upon, any particular place, the setting has no direct relationship to the drama being played, and a formal background of curtains is both adequate and satisfying.

A traverse curtain, which can be drawn across the stage about one-third of the distance between the footlights and

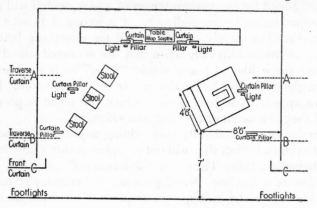

At end of Scene I   Close Curtain C

FIG. I. *King Lear:* ACT I, SCENE I

the back of the stage, is of considerable value, especially for Shakespearian production. Shakespeare's plays need to be played without intervals between the scenes, and in this the "traverse" assists. Usually, the scenes of these plays may be played alternately on the full stage and the smaller front part of the stage backed by the traverse curtain. A reading either of *The Merchant of Venice* or *Twelfth Night* will clearly indicate the practical possibility of this. The "traverse," however, does not serve merely as a convenient way of speeding up the production, for the scenes to be played on the front part of the stage gain by being acted on the smaller space. Usually, few characters are concerned and their dialogue is of an intimate nature.

Stage plots of a production of *King Lear*, played on a

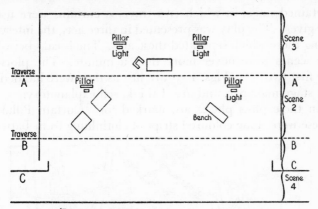

Scene 2 {Traverse A - closed   At end of scene - Open Traverse A
        {Traverse B - open

Scene 3 {Traverse A - open   At end of scene - Close Traverse B
        {Traverse B - open

At end of Scene 4 - Close Curtain C - End of Act I.

FIG. 2. *King Lear:* ACT I, SCENES 2, 3, and 4
(Scene 3 is Scenes 3 and 4 of the play; Scene 4 is Scene 5 of the play.)

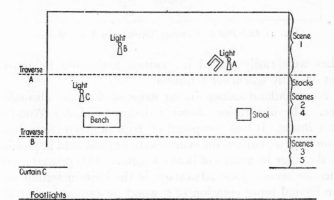

At end of Scene1 close traverse A and move off chair and 2 lights.
At end of Scene2   ·   ·   B
At end of Scene3 open   ·   B
At end of Scene4 close   ·   B and move off bench, stool and light.
At end of Scene5 open   ·   B on empty stage.
        Scene6   Empty Stage

FIG. 3. *King Lear:* ACT II, SCENES 1—4, AND ACT III, SCENES 1 and 2
(Scenes 5 and 6 above are Scenes 1 and 2 of Act III of the play.)

curtained stage, in which two traverse curtains were used, are given. The play was presented in three acts, the intervals being those which separated these acts. The breaks between the scenes were never more than a minute. The plots of the first two acts (Figs. 1–3) are just as they were handed to the stage manager, and are, I think, self-explanatory.

In these plots places are marked for "Curtain Pillars." These were stone coloured strips of cloth hung from battens.

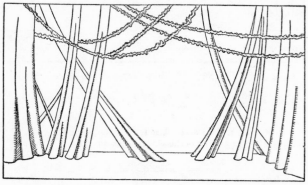

FIG. 4. *Dear Brutus:* CURTAIN DESIGN FOR LOB'S WOOD

They were easily placed in position and could be moved just as easily whenever required.

For woodland scenes similar strips of cloth are also effective. The illustration shows a design for Lob's Wood in *Dear Brutus.* It was composed of strips of green cloth, hung from battens, twisted into various shapes and held in position on the stage by means of heavy weights. This proved a very effective scene. One advantage of the curtain setting over the factual representation of a wood by canvas is that it is possible to have the pool, into which Margaret looks and which she uses as a mirror, at any convenient place for the actors, and not at a place dictated by the structure of the stage itself.

This set of curtains proved valuable in a production of *A Midsummer Night's Dream.* By varying the positions of the bases of the "trees," and the angles at which they sloped, different parts of the Wood near Athens were effectively illustrated.

The curtained stage with a traverse curtain may also be

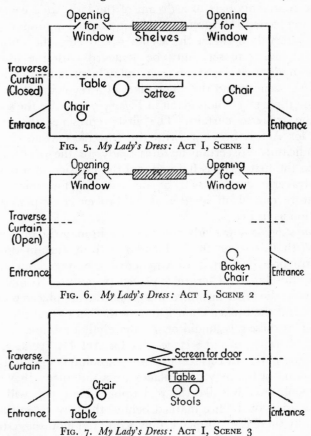

Fig. 5. *My Lady's Dress:* ACT I, SCENE 1

Fig. 6. *My Lady's Dress:* ACT I, SCENE 2

Fig. 7. *My Lady's Dress:* ACT I, SCENE 3

very effective for modern realistic drama. *My Lady's Dress,* by Edward Knoblock, is a play written in nine separate scenes, each of which takes place in a distinct locality and in different periods of time. Each scene has characters and incidents that are most realistic. The play opens in a lady's boudoir, moves to a peasant's house in Italy, a workshop in Lyons, a garden in Holland, an attic in Whitechapel, a trapper's stockade in Siberia, thence to a fashionable shop in New Bond-street, and back to the lady's boudoir. Each scene represents part of a dream of the lady we see in the opening scene. Interpretation demands speed in production; long intervals between the scenes would ruin the illusion. The changing of sets must be achieved with the utmost economy of time. How can such a play be produced without realistic scenery and the advantages of a revolving stage?

The three stage plots given in Figs. 5–7 indicate the value of the traverse curtain. The first represents the stage plot for Act I, Scene 1, with the traverse curtain closed. It indicates also certain features ready for the next scene. When the first scene is finished and the front curtain down, the traverse curtain will be opened, the four pieces of furniture moved off stage, and the broken chair placed in position as in Fig. 6.

The stage is now ready and the curtain may rise on Scene 2. With this scene finished and the front curtain down, the traverse curtain is drawn across the stage, but it is not quite closed; a screen is placed in position to make a doorway, the other furniture and properties are placed on the stage, and the broken chair is removed. The actual time for changing these sets should be less than half a minute.

Fig. 8 represents the stage plot for Act II, Scene 2, of the same play. In this scene a fire is absolutely essential for the action of the play. Fireplaces are a nuisance; they seldom look anything like the real thing. Here you will see the position of the fire marked behind the traverse curtain. Actually there is no fireplace, only a dull red light suggesting the fire.

In such a production of this play the changes in locality and period are carefully and adequately indicated by costume, the few pieces of furniture, and the stage properties. The attention of the audience is focused upon the actors and their language rather than on the accidental surroundings.

Play production is an interpretative and creative art; it should never be imitative. The vital problem for the producer is the translation of his mental images of the play and the characters into the symbols of his stage. The last two words must be strongly emphasized—*his* stage, not *the* stage.

It is an undoubted fact that while the stages mostly used by amateurs are small compared with those in the professional theatre, the measurements of furniture remain

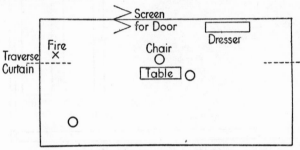

FIG. 8. *My Lady's Dress:* ACT II, SCENE 2.

constant. The attempt to copy a drawing-room as seen on a West End stage usually results in something comparable to a second-hand furniture emporium. It is unfortunate that, as the picture stage and the post-Ibsen naturalistic drama developed, the curtain became fallaciously known as the fourth wall of the room. This erroneous idea has led to the attempt to realize on the stage practically the whole of the floor space of every room shown. However successful this may have been in the professional theatre, it can lead only to cramp, dislocation, and often disaster on the stages used by many amateurs. Only that portion of a room vitally concerned with the action and necessary to give a symbol of reality should be attempted. The producer must strive to achieve interpretation with a minimum of furniture to secure a maximum of acting space.

It is not always advisable, and sometimes it is not possible, for amateurs to carry out the detailed descriptions of scenes given by an author. The description at the head of Act I, Scene 4, of *Children in Uniform* is "*Dormitory. Glaringly lighted white room, and six institutional iron white beds. At the back is a door into bathroom. One hears running water. . . .*"

I suppose we may at once "cut" the running water, but even then there remains the problem of six institutional iron white beds. Just try to imagine six beds on the platforms used for amateur shows! Work the problem for yourselves, and

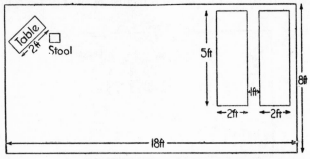

FIG. 9. *Children in Uniform:* ACT I, SCENE 4

realize how little room there would be left for the action of the play.

I recall an interesting performance of this play by a group of students on a platform measuring 18 ft. by 8 ft. Fig. 9 shows how the producer solved the problem of the six beds.

Here all the essentials of the dormitory are shown and good acting space is left. Members of the audience were readily able to imagine the other four beds in that part of the dormitory "off stage," and the dialogue made them aware when the children were in bed. This is a good example of imaginative use of a stage to interpret the author's intention by a creative use of stage symbols.

This splendid play for a large group of women presents a number of interesting problems for the producer and the actors. Act II, Scenes 1 and 3, take place in the Girls' Common Room. The only thing the author tells us about this room is that it contains a piano. From a reading of the two scenes, two things stand out clearly. First, the school-girls dance a waltz and a polka; second, these girls partake of a celebration supper. From this knowledge we are able to write down three conditions for these two scenes. We must have a piano, ample table space for the meal, and a large acting space for the dancing. Further study of Act II, Scene 3, compels concentration upon the closing moments of the scene. Manuela, the young schoolgirl, blissfully drunk, is sottishly confiding to her twelve schoolmates that one of the mistresses—Fraulein von Bernburg—loves her. She knows because the schoolmistress has given her one of her chemises to wear. The other children, who have now become aware of the presence of the Head Mistress, listen in amazement as Manuela, smiling blissfully upon them, continues—

Nothing can happen to me now—nothing can touch me—nothing in the whole world . . . she loves me ! I know it—I feel it—it gives me strength—it makes me feel holy. . . . From now on I will be quite different, I will have only good pure thoughts . . . and I will serve her . . . life has no other meaning. . . .

At this moment Manuela for the first time catches sight of the Head Mistress, who has been standing transfixed, listening to the emotional ramblings of the drunken school-girl. There is a pause as Manuela tries to grasp the situation. Then she takes up a glass of wine, and shouts—

To our beloved, glorious, wonderful Fraulein von Bernburg ! Long may she live !

Manuela staggers and falls fainting to the ground.

For this climax to be realized upon the stage it is essential to focus attention upon both the protagonists; Manuela and the Head Mistress. The audience must be readily aware of both, and at the same time it must be contrived that these two, separately, and the rest of the children may play their parts in the crisis. This climax adds a fourth condition for the setting of the scene, namely, an entrance to the stage that will be a focus of interest and at the same time unobtrusive to those playing on the stage.

It will be observed that the four conditions are fulfilled in this plan. There are a piano, a large table, a large acting space, and an entrance by which the Head Mistress will at once be in a position of interest to the audience while remaining unseen by those playing for as long as we wish.

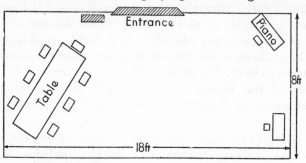

FIG. 10. *Children in Uniform:* ACT II, SCENE 3.

The furniture inevitably leads the eye to this entrance and clearly indicates where both the Head Mistress and Manuela will be positioned for the climax of the scene. The desk, the small table, the stools round the table, and at the piano and desk, were added later.

Now, recall the famous scene in *The School for Scandal*—the scene in which Lady Teazle visits Joseph Surface and is finally discovered behind the screen by her husband, Sir Peter. The only essentials for this are the screen and two chairs, and, before anything else is added, careful consideration must be given to the screen.

It is of interest immediately the curtain rises, for we see the unusual sight of a screen covered with maps. To make sure that the audience takes heed, very early reference is made to the screen and a servant is required to move it. When Lady Teazle is hiding behind it, Sir Peter remarks—

and you can even make your screen a source of knowledge.

The screen is of interest throughout, but when Sir Peter

spies the petticoat of the lady behind it, it at once becomes
the focus of interest, which accumulates, and finally, in a
struggle between Sir Peter Teazle and Charles Surface, the
screen is thrown down and Lady Teazle stands revealed.
Here is the culminating moment of the scene, the moment
which must be impressed upon the minds of the audience.
It is the climax, and the high pitch of excitement must be
maintained from this moment to the closing words of the
scene.

Now in actual life this screen might fall anywhere; on
the stage it must be made to fall in a seemingly natural
manner, but it must be so contrived that afterwards it is
out of the way—out of the consciousness of the audience and
in such a position that it will not inconvenience any desired
movement on the part of the actors. Many performances of
this scene have been ruined at its most interesting point
because the producer has not realized that a particular
space measuring at least 6 ft. by 1 ft. 6 in. must be planned
for the fallen screen.

One could describe performances where the screen has
completely blocked the exit from the stage, where the screen
has not fallen to the ground because of a table in the way,
or where the screen has collapsed on to Lady Teazle, knock-
ing her hat over her eyes. But let attention rather be concentrated on the more practical and constructive thought
arising out of consideration of this scene. Does it not indicate, exactly as did those scenes from *Children in Uniform*,
that in planning a scene the essential requirements should
first be noted, and that the greatest care should be given to
the requirements for the climax?

Sheridan places this scene in a library, and the Drury
Lane scene depicted a magnificent factual library complete
with hundreds of dummy books on painted shelves. It was
a most admirable feat on the part of the stage carpenters and
painters, but the effort was futile, as neither the characters
nor the incidents were in any way concerned with this display
of paint and canvas.

SUMMARY

1. Modern theorists and the drama.
2. A play is concerned with characters and their story as revealed to an audience by actors.
3. The only essentials for dramatic presentation are an acting space, an auditorium, and actors.
4. The formal background.
5. The background of the actor should be of interest through him and not for its own sake.
6. Setting for a play should be planned in relation to the work of the actors.
7. Very few scenes demand factual representation of background.
8. Screens as a stage background.
9. Curtain settings.
10. A traverse curtain.
11. Stage plots for a production of *King Lear* to illustrate the use of the traverse curtain.
12. The use of curtains for woodland scenes.
13. The traverse curtain and modern realistic drama.
14. Setting a stage.
15. Play production is an interpretative and creative art; it should never be imitative.
16. The producer should strive to achieve interpretation with a minimum of furniture to secure a maximum of acting space.
17. The vital problem for the producer is the translation of his mental images of the play and the characters into the symbols of *his* stage.
18. Conditions for staging imposed upon the producer by the dramatist in scenes from *Children in Uniform*.
19. Conditions imposed by the Screen Scene in *The School for Scandal*.
20. In planning a scene the essential requirements should first be noted, and the greatest care should be given to the requirements for the climax.

EXERCISES ON CHAPTER IX

1. *Mourning Becomes Electra*, by Eugene O'Neill.

In this play there is a psychological significance in the architecture that affects the characters of the play, and at the same time exerts an emotional influence on the audience. Architecture is an integral part of the play.

Would it be possible to produce this play on a curtained stage? Could it be produced against a background of screens? If so, how would you suggest the significance of the house planned in the style of a Greek temple?

2. *The Kingdom of God*, by Sierra.

Plan screen settings for the scenes of this play.

3. *Call it a Day*, by Dodie Smith.

It is essential that the intervals between the scenes of this play shall be short. Write a list of essential furniture for each scene. How can the laborious and lengthy task of changing pieces of furniture be avoided?

4. *My Lady's Dress*, by Edward Knoblock.

Make stage plots for Acts II and III of this play. Use a minimum of furniture and the traverse curtain as indicated in the plots given for Act 1.

5. *Escape*, by John Galsworthy.

You are required to produce this play on a curtained stage. How can you make effective use of a traverse curtain? How can you suggest change of locality?

6. *Mrs. Moonlight*, by Benn W. Levy.

Write lists of essential furniture for each act. How will you show the passing of time between the acts?

7. *The Silver Box*, by John Galsworthy: Act III. London Police Court.

It is interesting to compare the stage setting of this scene with that necessary for the Trial Scene of *The Merchant of Venice*. Plan a setting and give reasons for your plan.

8. *They Came to a City*, by J. B. Priestley.

Read the Note on the Set prefacing the play, and then try to arrange sets by using only screens or curtains.

9. *The Rose and Crown*, by J. B. Priestley.

The set for this play is defined as the Public Bar of the Rose and Crown. How will you place this bar so that in a small hall, where all the seats are below stage level, the beer engines will not mask the players?

CHAPTER X

PLAY PRODUCTION: GROUPING AND MOVEMENT

IT cannot be too strongly emphasized that play production is an interpretative and creative art, and that it should never be imitative. The common practice of accepting and following the numerous stage directions given in many printed copies of modern plays is bad. To direct an actor to move over to a settee placed left centre merely because this is an instruction in the printed copy, or to "rise and take up hat" merely because of a parenthetical phrase in the special edition for amateur actors, can result only in a performance that lacks vitality and purpose. A great actor of the past urged that all punctuation marks should be erased from an actor's script. Most certainly all stage directions should be expunged from the producer's copy of the play to be rehearsed.

The grouping and movement of characters upon a stage should be aids to the interpretation and communication of a play to an audience. The producer must be aware of his stage and have definite mental images of the scenes he wishes to be communicated. It is as important for him to arrange the grouping and the movements as it is to select and place the furniture and properties for his stage. Groupings and movements should not depend upon the dictates of any authority, no matter how great, but should always be planned to assist in the interpretation and in the communication of the conceptions of the play in the mind of the producer. There can be no spectacle sadder than that of the so-called producer who sits or stands in front of the stage and controls a rehearsal by repeating the instructions found in the printed copy: "Now, put your hat and stick on chair above writing-table, and come down left of Lady Stick-in-the-mud." "Now you will move up stage and open window. I am not sure if we shall be able to have a window, but, never mind, that will do for the moment, and if we can't have a window, well, you will have to—er—well just move up to where the window ought to be."

Grouping must be an aid to interpretation. It is not sufficient for the characters merely to look well as they are grouped about the stage. The idea that pictorial effect is all that is desired in stage grouping has led to many otherwise well-rehearsed scenes going wrong "on the night."

A study of a scene from *Henry IV*, Part 1, will deepen

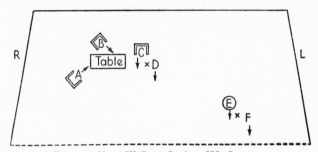

Fig. 11. *Henry IV*, Part I: Act III, Scene 1
(A, Worcester; B, Glendower; C, Lady Mortimer; D, Mortimer;
E, Lady Percy; F, Hotspur.)

understanding of this very important principle. In Act III, Scene 1, the following characters are on the stage: Hotspur, Worcester, Mortimer, Glendower, Lady Percy, and Lady Mortimer. Lady Mortimer is Welsh, and can speak only that language. During the latter part of the scene she is called upon to sing in Welsh. A plot of the stage, setting out positions for the characters, is given above.

At once it will be seen that here is a pleasing picture. The stage is well-balanced, the characters are grouped round the principal protagonist, Lady Mortimer, who is about to sing. Yet in the performance, the audience, instead of listening to the song, will most probably be interested in the figure of Hotspur and the song will probably be ruined by laughter. It will be distressing to all concerned on the stage. The lady may sing beautifully. All the other characters may remain perfectly quiet and interested, yet the probability is the audience will not be able to refrain from laughter at the sight of the fiery Hotspur, lying at the feet of Lady Percy, bored by being compelled to listen to a Welsh song he cannot understand. What will cause this distraction? Why will interest turn to Hotspur when the song should claim it?

Study the grouping closely and you will see that actually there are two distinct and separate groups. There is the one consisting of Worcester, Glendower, Welsh Lady, and Mortimer, with the Welsh Lady as the focus of interest; and

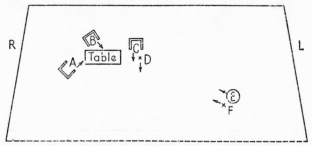

FIG. 12. *Henry IV*, PART I: ACT III, SCENE I—SUGGESTED PLOT

there is also the group of Lady Percy and Hotspur with no link to connect it with the former. The fact that Hotspur is already a great favourite with the audience and that no other character on the stage has played such an important part as he, naturally causes the audience to give him their attention just at the moment when he should be able to subside into relative unimportance. The method of grouping, together with the popularity of Hotspur already established, combine to make him the focus of interest, and the slight boredom suggested by him causes laughter and destroys the effect desired.

It is of the greatest importance that everything on the stage shall direct attention towards the particular point of interest at each moment of the play. Above I give a plot for this scene that will avoid the trouble and focus attention upon the singer throughout this episode.

You will see that the only change made is the direction in which Lady Percy and Hotspur face. Now there is only one group upon the stage. All the characters are directing attention towards the proper focus of interest. Even if the popularity of Hotspur claims briefly the attention of any section of the audience, the directing lines of his limbs, and the direction of the gaze both of Hotspur and Lady Percy, will inevitably cause the audience to look towards the lady who is about to sing. In the former illustration interest wavers between the two groups, and finally rests with the character whose personality dominates the play; in the latter illustration the focus of interest at this particular moment of the play is firmly established and will be maintained so long as the Lady singing is worth listening to.

Here is the fundamental principle for grouping characters on a stage. If this constructive and positive principle is observed, there will be little danger of scenes going wrong "on the night."

Grouping and movement are essential elements in the drama. They must be determined from the play itself, and not be the result either of accident or of a desire for variety. The purpose of moving and grouping characters must always be to reveal the significance of the text.

The purpose of Act II, Scene 3, of *Children in Uniform* is to develop the story of Manuela, to show her at the moment of her great triumph and her degradation. Everything done in this scene must direct attention to her.

As the curtain rises, Johanna and two girls are laying the table in preparation for a celebration supper, and at the same time we hear the words of a play which other schoolchildren are acting "off stage." Immediately, the three characters on the stage stop laying the table to listen to the play. They are "entranced" as they listen to the words, and they are "thrilled" as they hear the great applause. They finish laying the table, but all their talk and their interest is in the performance of the play, and especially that of Manuela.

Movement and grouping in the opening of this scene are,

of course, partly determined by the need for laying the table, but they are principally concerned with directing attention to Manuela. The attention of the audience must be directed towards her, and not to that which is happening on the stage. The audience will watch the table being laid, but their conscious interest must be with the girls acting "off stage."

Actually this moment serves as an introduction to the scene itself. Nothing that takes place on the stage is really of any importance for itself. It is not essential for the audience to witness the laying of the table; it will not matter if they have forgotten all about it when the play is finished. Amateurs sensing the unimportance of laying the table sometimes think it matters little how it is done. Unfortunately, the surest way to make such a moment stand out in the minds of the audience is to do the business carelessly and indifferently. Only by great precision in their movements will these three actresses be able to achieve their purpose. The most trivial error, the slightest mistake in "timing," or an accidental movement will cause the attention of the audience to be concentrated on those on the stage, and Manuela will for that moment be forgotten.

Following this introduction, these three characters leave the stage and Manuela enters, followed by Ilse.

Frequently the grouping and moving of two characters are treated most casually. It seems to be assumed that little care or plan is necessary when only a few characters are on the stage. Often we see two characters standing in the middle of the stage, like two duet singers, each in turn facing the audience to say his part; or each taking a corner of the platform and speaking across the proscenium opening as if each was a corner man in a minstrel show. Recently I watched the rehearsal of a play in which two characters were together in several scenes. The producer made no comment with regard to position or movement, so in each scene Mr. A took up his position in the centre of the stage, and Mr. B stood down right. During the rehearsal of the third scene, the producer suddenly thought a change was desirable and asked, "Mr. A, don't you think, as you have been in the centre in the other two scenes, you might let Mr. B go there in this one?"

Some years ago I saw a performance of *The Merchant of Venice*. In Act II, Scene 8, the actors playing Salarino and Salanio evidently thought movement to be essential, so at regular intervals they changed places!

In this scene of *Children in Uniform* there is the instruction that Manuela enters, followed by Ilse. This may be a literal description of what happens, but it certainly does not indicate how it happens. A moment's reflection brings realization that they do not come to the Common Room by mutual arrangement. Manuela rushes there when she comes "off stage" to get away from her companions. She does not expect or hope to meet Ilse there. Ilse, who has been sitting in the audience, sees Manuela and follows her in order that she can be the first to congratulate her upon her performance. The entrances of these two must indicate the separate and individual reasons for entering the Common Room. There must be just a sufficient lapse of time between their entrances to make these motives effective; to enable Manuela to express her appreciation of her solitude, and to demonstrate her surprise as she turns to see Ilse. Manuela certainly rushes to the Common Room, but once there she leisurely walks into the room and probably towards the desk down left, on which she may place her helmet. Ilse not only rushes to, but across the Common Room until she reaches Manuela.

The intimate dialogue which follows naturally keeps them close together. The movement and gesture, which accompany this dialogue, must emphasize the varying moods and thoughts of Manuela. Ilse is of interest only because she is instrumental in causing Manuela to display her yearning to hear sympathetic comment by Fraulein von Bernburg. The movement during this little episode must assist in the development towards its own climax, which is the elation on Manuela's face as Ilse says—

But she looked, my dear. Oh, she looked. . . . Her eyes.

During this episode, which lasts only a moment or two, Manuela passes through many swiftly changing moods, which are the result of excitement and highly-strung nerves. These moods affect her movements, which must be planned to enable the audience to appreciate her thoughts, her anger, her despair, and her elation. The relation of the movements of Manuela to those of Ilse must be contrived so that Manuela is always the focus of interest. Position and movement must be definite and precise in order that the right emphasis may be given to character and emotion.

The grouping and moving of characters on the stage are as important as is "composition" in painting. The purpose in an artist's mind influences his disposition of the details of his picture, the intensity of light and shade, and the selection of his colours. By the grouping and moving of his actors the producer gives emphasis to character and point to a scene.

The purpose of the Trial Scene (Act IV, Scene 1) of *The Merchant of Venice* lies in the conflict between Shylock and Portia. While it is true that the trial takes place in a Court of Justice, and before that most important dignitary, the Duke of Venice, it is equally true that neither the Court nor the Duke plays an important role in the issue of the trial. Actually, if either was, or both were, eliminated the dramatic power of the scene would be unimpaired. It is not my wish to eliminate the Duke; he has some purpose in the trial, but it is very important that his dignity and magnificence should not be imposed upon the scene to the detraction of the greater issue.

There is a strong temptation to set the Duke's throne at "centre back" of the stage. On a very large stage, where it is possible to build a throne high above the level of the platform, or in a theatre where most of the audience looks down upon the stage, this may be an appropriate position. But on a smaller stage, and in a hall where the greater part of the audience is seated below the level of the platform, this point of the stage must almost inevitably be an important focus of interest. Seated at "centre back" of the stage, robed in his brilliant costume, the Duke must always attract much attention.

On any but very large stages, the Duke must be placed somewhere at the side so that he may always be an interested spectator; so that other characters may address him and the audience at the same time; so that he may direct attention to the particular characters of importance; and so that he may be prevented from superimposing his civic importance upon the scene's significant purpose.

Let us now concentrate attention upon the moment of crisis—

> Tarry a little; there is something else.

The first three words stay Shylock at the very moment when the greatest desire of his soul is about to be attained. For him, and all present in that Court, these words seem to arrest "time." All is hushed and still. The words

> There is something else

arouse attention and hope that has been frustrated for so long. Portia proceeds and hope becomes realized joy. It surely is of some significance that, right through this crisis, until some time after Portia has delivered her final judgment, Antonio, who seemingly should be most concerned, plays no direct or active part. The only distraction from Portia and Shylock comes from Gratiano, whose taunts are as vinegar in open wounds, and emphasize the suffering of the Jew.

Shakespeare, seemingly, would have all the emphasis of this climax placed on Shylock, and none on Antonio. Yet we know that Antonio and Bassanio must in their individual ways be feeling emotions of the utmost relief and joy. Quite easily the very calmness of this joy can become the supreme *motif* of the moment. But it must not. The grouping of the actors must give emphasis to Shylock and his complete downfall. Antonio and Bassanio are difficult characters to place in this scene. Both are interesting figures, especially Bassanio, who has already established himself as a favourite with the audience.

The problem we have here is very similar to the one we had in *Henry IV*, and similarly must it be solved. The positions of the characters at this moment of the climax must recognize the conditions and focus attention upon Shylock and secondarily upon Portia.

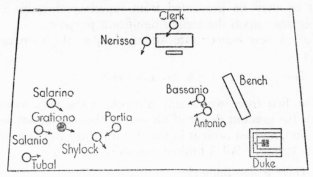

FIG. 13. *The Merchant of Venice:* ACT IV, SCENE I

Fig. 13 shows a stage plot which fulfils the conditions of this scene. The positions of Antonio and Bassanio need explanation. Antonio is standing with his body towards Bassanio, his arms are supported by Bassanio, but his head is turned so that he looks over his left shoulder towards Shylock. Bassanio, similarly, is standing with his body towards Antonio, while he looks across at Portia and Shylock. All the other characters are facing Shylock, whose slight inward turn helps to give interest to Portia.

It is not suggested that these positions are the only ones for an interpretation of this moment. There are many ways of achieving the same result. But the climax of a play must be realized. The climax is the most important moment of a scene. It is the moment, above all others, that must be impressed upon the audience, for it establishes the purpose of the scene or play.

Everything done in a scene should lead up to the climax. All movements must be arranged so that they will inevitably lead the actors to their right positions for this supreme moment. To achieve this it is of the first importance for a producer to decide upon the climax of the scene being interpreted, to fix positions to ensure the proper communication of this moment, then to arrange all previous movements and positions. The producer must know where he is leading his actors before he determines the road upon which they shall travel.

SUMMARY

1. The grouping and movement of characters upon a stage should be aids to the interpretation and communication of a play to an audience.

2. It is not sufficient that the characters shall look well as they are grouped about the stage.

3. Importance of the focus of interest.

4. Everything on a stage should direct attention towards the particular point of interest at each moment of a play.

5. The purpose of moving and grouping characters is to reveal the significance of the text.

6. Grouping and movement must be determined from the play itself, and not be the result of accident or a desire for variety.

7. By the grouping and moving of his actors, the producer will give emphasis to character and point to a scene.

8. *The Merchant of Venice.* The Trial Scene.

    (a) Relation of the Duke to the purpose of the scene.

    (b) Consideration of the climax.

9. The climax of a play must be realized.

10. Everything done on the stage must lead up to the climax.

EXERCISES ON CHAPTER X

1. *Berkeley Square,* by John Balderston: Act I, Scene 3.

The opening of this scene provides an interesting study of two characters on the stage.

Delete all stage directions from your copy, then, from a study of the dialogue and your appreciation of the personalities of Peter and Kate, and from your knowledge of previous circumstances, work out positions and movements during their dialogue.

Observe that, at the beginning, interest is shared equally, but that, when Kate invites Peter to sit, interest becomes focused upon Peter. Then once again interest becomes shared as their conversation turns on the subject of how Peter got into the house, and during his enforced formal proposal.

2. Continue your study of the above scene to the entrance of Lady Anne and the entrances of Helen, Throstle, and Tom.

Again try not to take notice of the instructions or diagrams given in your copy of the play. Try to work out positions and movements for yourself. If you will do this, you will readily observe that the final positions of Kate and Peter, before the entrance of Lady Anne, are dependent upon the position of the door for the entrance of the Lady, and also upon the positions taken up by Helen and Throstle immediately after their entrance.

This is not a difficult scene to plan, but it clearly indicates the need for definite planning and purposeful movement.

3. *Julius Caesar:* Act IV, Scene 3. The dialogue between Cassius and Brutus beginning—

That you have wrong'd me doth appear in this.

Movement in a scene of this kind is of considerable emotional importance. There is frequently a tendency for it to be haphazard; it should be studied and purposeful. Movement made at wrong moments during a passionate scene may cause interest to become diffused. The movements in this scene must be planned as carefully as those in a love scene.

4. *The Merchant of Venice:* Act III, Scene 2.

Plan the movements of Bassanio and Portia from the moment he discovers the picture of Portia in the leaden casket.

Remember that organized, controlled, and purposeful movement will be an aid to sincerity and spontaneity.

5. *Berkeley Square:* Act II.

This act provides fascinating exercises in grouping and movement. Always there must be a pleasing pictorial interest about the various groupings, even when only two characters are on the stage, but there must also be purpose in the groups and the movement. Focus of interest changes frequently, yet all moves inevitably towards the climax of the scene; from the opening dialogue interest is aroused in the affinity existing between Peter and Helen.

The grouping and movement during the appearance of the Duke of Cumberland are difficult and complicated. During this episode the movement must be as controlled as dance movement is controlled.

6. *Twelfth Night:* Act V.

A difficult scene to plan because of the continually changing interests. Nevertheless, when it is planned with care, focusing attention upon each successive point of interest, it is a scene which becomes impressive by reason of its humour, pathos, and romance.

There are no stage directions other than those that are found as the dialogue is searched. Imagination is not hedged in by parenthetical notes. There is freedom to build in accordance with wishes.

Arrange a grouping of the characters for the moment when Sebastian greets Olivia. Then try to develop movement up to this picture, and also the scene from this point.

7. *Mrs. Moonlight*, by Benn W. Levy: Act III.

Plan a stage and the positions of the characters for the climax of this scene.

8. *The Lady with a Lamp*, by Reginald Berkeley. Act I.

Grouping and movement are extremely interesting problems in this scene. It is important that the grouping shall suggest the intimacy of an English home, and the friendliness of polite discussion. During the early part Lord Palmerston is of peculiar interest, but the focus of interest ultimately falls upon Florence. Keep this in mind as the positions of the terrace furniture are planned.

9. *The Lady with a Lamp*: Act I, Scene 2.

The dialogue between Florence and Tremayne presents an interesting problem in movement.

There are two characters and the fountain, which is invested with personality by the dialogue. The fountain has a fixed position, which becomes a focus of interest at given moments during the scene. But, ultimately, the interest focuses upon the two lovers and, finally, upon Florence as she visualizes the future.

All the movements of this scene must be planned to emphasize the sincerity of these two great souls, and the depth of the emotional and spiritual feeling of Florence.

10. *Julius Caesar*: Act III, Scene 1.

Plan movements of the characters during this scene. Some points to note—

(a) Position of the body of Caesar during the latter part of the scene.

(b) Position of Caesar when he is struck.

(c) Order in which characters strike Caesar.

(d) Positions of conspirators before they stab Caesar and after the stabbing.

(e) Caesar is throughout the scene the focus of interest.

11. *Will Shakespeare*, by Clemence Dane: Act I. The movement of the players representing the "shadows" of characters from the plays of Shakespeare.

The stage must be made to seem full of indistinct, shadowy figures and movement. At intervals, one or other well-known character emerges into the full light and claims the attention of the audience; at other times attention must be focused either upon Anne or upon Will Shakespeare. Treat this section of the scene in a simple manner, but keep the whole moving.

Lighting will play an interesting part in this scene.

12. *Dear Brutus*, by J. M. Barrie: Act 1. From the entrance of Lob and his visitors just before Dearth discovers that the garden is now the Wood.

The grouping and movement of the characters in this part of the scene are rather complicated, because the purpose of the characters in it conflict with what is to take place, and the discovery of the Wood arrests them from their intentions. Those on the stage are completely surprised by the discovery; even Lob is thrilled.

Note. The aspiring producer cannot practise grouping and moving characters too assiduously. It is a skill as well as an art.

CHAPTER XI

Play Production: Purpose and Climax

E VERY play has a central theme or purpose. Each scene or part has its own special motive which illuminates, or helps to establish, this main purpose. The dramatist has selected his characters, their dialogue, and the incidents for their appropriateness in elaborating and emphasizing the idea that has dominated and inspired his writing.

What is the main purpose of Shaw's *Pygmalion*? In his preface the playwright says: "The reformer England needs to-day is an energetic phonetic enthusiast: that is why I have made such a one the hero of a popular play." Henry Higgins, a professor of phonetics, teaches Eliza Doolittle to speak English perfectly, and to behave in a lady-like manner. In Act V we discover that he has achieved something more. Out of the "draggletailed guttersnipe" we met under the portico of Covent Garden, he has created a new being, a creature in his own image.

In simple terms the theme of *Pygmalion* may be stated as A SCIENTIST CREATES.

Realization of this theme compels the producer to concentrate upon the Professor as the principal character. The theme concerns him and his creation. He is the central figure, and Eliza Doolittle is the chief secondary character— the clay into which he breathes the spirit of a new life.

This play's purpose can be established in the minds of the audience only when the performance focuses attention upon and emphasizes the CLIMAX: that moment in the play when the dramatist finally asserts the idea to which all that happens has been leading. The climax of *Pygmalion* is to be found towards the end of the last act, when Eliza suddenly realizes her power and complete equality with Professor Higgins, and when, at the same time, Higgins awakens to the fact that he has realized his dream.

Hitherto Eliza has been dominated and at times tortured by Higgins. She has been aware of her own knowledge, but has not understood its implication. Now she becomes alive to the full significance of her own power and tells Higgins that she will teach what he has taught her. At the moment of her great discovery she cries—

> Oh, when I think of myself crawling under your feet and being trampled on and called names, when all the time I had only to lift my finger to be as good as you, I could just kick myself.

Higgins gazes at her in wonder. Here is the new creature he has striven to create. He is deeply moved as he appreciates the magnitude of his achievement. His ecstasy is intense as from the depths of his great mind he says—

> You damned impudent slut, you! But it's better than snivelling; better than fetching slippers and finding spectacles, isn't it? *By George, Eliza, I said I'd make a woman of you; and I have. I like you like this.*

Here is the climax. AN ENERGETIC PHONETIC ENTHUSIAST HAS REFORMED A HUMAN BEING. By his power as a teacher, and through his scientific knowledge, he has created a new being. The play's purpose is to demonstrate this idea. The producer must do his utmost to establish this purpose in the minds of the audience, and to achieve this he must ensure that the various scenes lead up to the final climax.

Let us see how the play leads towards this final goal. A study of each separate act suggests the following—

Act I.   THE SCIENTIST STATES HIS VISION.

            The climax is the actual statement of the ability to reform Eliza.

Act II.   THE SCIENTIST ACCEPTS THE OPPORTUNITY TO ACHIEVE HIS VISION.

            Climax is in the last two speeches of the scene.

Act III.   THE SCIENTIST DISPLAYS HIS UNFINISHED PRODUCT, AND A PROBLEM IS STATED.

The true climax of this scene is the statement of the problem by Mrs. Higgins.

Act IV. DISAPPOINTMENT IN SUCCESS AND THE PROBLEM UNSOLVED.

Climax is the last speech.

Act V. Triumph and realization of victory. THE CREATION OF A NEW BEING.

Frequently performances of this play tend to break down at the end of the third act. Interest accumulates during Acts I and II and reaches its highest pitch of excitement during the third act, at Eliza's exit. From this point interest wanes. On several occasions I have heard it said that the play could quite well finish at the exit of Eliza, and that the last two acts are unnecessary.

Such a feeling can be the result only of a production concentrating upon Eliza Doolittle rather than upon the Professor. In the third act, while this young woman is on the stage she is undoubtedly the central figure. She is being exhibited so that her teacher may note the effect she will make upon those present at the exhibition. But it should be noted, and made clear in performance, that even while Higgins is in the background he maintains an influence over Eliza and signals instructions to her. She is his "exhibit." She is the focus of interest. Both to those on the stage and to the audience she is most fascinating, and her exit is one of the most startling in dramatic literature. All the time she is on the stage she claims the attention of an audience that is thrilled, and excitement becomes intense.

But, sensational as her exit is, it is not the climax of the scene. For a space there is a lull in the excitement, but gradually the scene takes on fresh interest and Shaw provides a "duet" between Higgins and Pickering which, for dramatic brilliance, has never been surpassed. Something extraordinary had to be done to reclaim the interest of the audience after their recent excitement. To achieve this, Shaw provided this original method. Higgins and Pickering are naturally excited after the events portrayed, and Shaw uses their excitement for his dramatic purpose in this wonderful "duet." Then he silences them, and also the audience, in preparation for the most important moment when Mrs. Higgins tells them of the "problem of what is to be done with her afterwards."

The importance of this "duet" of Higgins and Pickering cannot be over-stressed. Properly done, its effect is tumultuous, and the surrender of the audience is complete. By this master-stroke Shaw recaptures the audience's interest and prepares the way for the climax of the scene, and for the development of the theme of the play. When the "duet" is rehearsed until it is dramatically perfect, the play cannot "break" at the exit of Eliza, for there will be eager anticipation of subsequent happenings.

Eugene O'Neill clearly states the purpose of each section of his trilogy, *Mourning Becomes Electra*. This tragedy embodies, in modern psychological terms, a conception of Nemesis and Retribution. It is divided into three separate and complete tragedies: "Homecoming," "The Hunted," and "The Haunted." Yet the whole is a continuous, sustained theme that moves forward to its inevitable Fate.

Rudolf Besier similarly states the purpose of each act of *The Barretts of Wimpole Street*. His titles focus attention on the main incident or character of each section. Act I: "Porter in a Tankard"; Act II: "Mr. Robert Browning"; Act III: "Robert"; Act IV: "Henrietta"; Act V: "Papa." These titles are the clearest sign-posts for the producer and the actors. What a nice and suggestive distinction there is between the titles for Acts II and III !

When the final speech is correctly "timed," and spoken with appropriate tones, the climax of this play is magnificent comedy. At this moment the last petty tyranny of "Papa" is thwarted.

For a number of reasons, upon which I will not speculate, amateur performances rarely emphasize the purpose of a play or make enough of its climax. Individual performances of considerable merit are common; moments of intense emotional power and humorous quality are realized; but only occasionally are the play's essential moments seized upon and stressed so that an audience becomes more absorbed in the play than in the actors. Yet this should be the aim of all performances.

Frequently, I think, actors themselves are more interested in their own performances than they are in the play. Perhaps this is natural. Indeed, it may be essential. It is certainly the actor's duty to interpret his character and to play his allotted part to the utmost of his ability. It is the producer's business to see that the play itself is appropriately interpreted and its theme properly developed. The producer must see that the various characters, incidents, and dialogue are stressed so that their relative importance may be appreciated, and their special purpose in the general pattern of the play understood.

The first—and probably the most important—task of a producer is to decide on the purpose and climax of the play he is about to produce. He must also decide upon the climaxes and the various sub-climaxes of each separate scene which direct attention and lead towards the supreme moment of the play.

Each scene in a Shakespearian play has its special purpose in the development of the dramatic scheme. Sometimes a scene develops the story, at others it directs attention to some special character, or serves to stress a particular dramatic conflict. Whatever the individual purpose may be, it is the producer's and the actors' task to emphasize it. The purpose is not always single. Sometimes there may be a dual purpose, as in Act I, Scene 3, of *The Merchant of Venice*. In this scene there is the dual purpose of focusing attention upon the conflict between Antonio and Shylock and the drawing up of the bond upon which the rest of the play is developed. Each of these purposes must be stressed so that the audience may follow the subsequent movement of the play.

It should be realized that an audience is capable of retaining only a limited number of impressions of any performance. The whole of a play cannot be retained in its memory, even for a short time, after seeing the performance. This fact alone makes it imperative that the actors should clearly appreciate which are to be the moments of a play that must be stressed in order that it may be best appreciated. These moments must receive careful rehearsal so that they will stand out in performance. If these climaxes are acted with due regard for their relative values, then it may be that the play will be well received and understood.

Emphasis and stress are as important in production as they are in the individual performances of characters, and in the rendering of single speeches and sentences. Proper attention to emphasis in production gives rhythm to the development and movement of a play, and this rhythm is one of the chief factors in controlling attention and retaining interest. When everything in the production is evenly stressed, the result is monotonous, interest wanes, and attention is diffused. When stress is badly placed, and minor points are out of focus, the minds of the audience tend to become confused and muddled. Interest can be sustained only when all the details are given their true values, and this can be achieved only by appropriate emphasis in the acting.

Players are often disturbed because the opening scene or scenes are not received with quite the hoped-for enthusiasm. They should remind themselves of the dramatic purpose of these scenes. Usually they serve only to introduce characters and the theme of the play. There is no reason why such scenes should arouse anything more than an interest of curiosity. The audience is behaving quite properly in receiving these introductions calmly and quietly. Upon such a quiet beginning a highly successful performance may be developed. This is especially true of all the best plays in our literature, and the actors should be more seriously alarmed when an audience rises at once to enthusiastic appreciation than when it attends with quiet dignity to the dramatist's

carefully-laid plans. Some of the best productions I have
known have begun thus quietly.

Obviously, a good dramatist knows his job. He knows how
to construct his play so that his purpose in writing it shall
be understood. Do not try to improve upon his work. Just
seek out his intentions and bring them before the audience.
This applies equally to language, character, incident, and
the play as a whole. Find the words, the characters, and the
incidents the playwright would have you stress, discover the
purpose underlying each detail, give your attention to these,
and leave the rest to him.

SUMMARY

1. Every play has a central theme or purpose.
2. The main purpose of Shaw's *Pygmalion*.
3. The purpose of the play can be established in the minds
of the audience only when the performance focuses attention
on and emphasizes the climax.
4. The climax of *Pygmalion*.
5. The purposes of each separate act of *Pygmalion*.
6. The climax of Act III of *Pygmalion*.
7. The importance of the duet of Professor Higgins and
Colonel Pickering.
8. *Mourning Becomes Electra*.
9. *The Barretts of Wimpole Street*.
10. Actors are frequently more interested in individual
performances than in the play.
11. The importance of the climax.
12. Each scene of a Shakespearian play has its own special
purpose.
13. An audience is capable of retaining only a limited number
of impressions. The important moments are the climaxes.
14. Emphasis and stress are as important in production as
they are in the individual performances of characters.
15. Quiet beginnings.

EXERCISES ON CHAPTER XI

1. *The Barretts of Wimpole Street*, by Rudolf Besier.
Find reasons for the titles given by Rudolf Besier to each act. What
are the climaxes of each act?

2. *Mourning Becomes Electra*, by Eugene O'Neill.
Give reasons for the titles of each part of Eugene O'Neill's trilogy.

State the climaxes of each scene. Show from the text the influence of the House upon the characters.

3. State the purpose of each scene of *Twelfth Night*. State the climax of each scene.

4. *The School for Scandal*, by Sheridan.

What is the purpose of this play? What are the climaxes of each scene?

5. *The Ship*, by St. John Ervine.

What is the purpose of this modern tragedy?

Show how each scene leads to the climax of the play.

6. *Riders to the Sea*, by J. M. Synge.

What is the climax of this great one-act play?

How will the producer establish this climax?

7. *The Sleeping Clergyman*, by James Bridie.

What is the dramatic significance of the Clergyman?

How can this significance be established in performance?

What is the climax of the play, and what are the various climaxes of each scene?

How can these be impressed upon the audience?

8. *The Burning Glass*, by Charles Morgan.

The author gives only different times for each of the four scenes of this play. Find the climax of each scene, and state in one sentence, if possible, the purpose of each scene and the whole play. Are the times really significant and, if so, in what way?

9. *The Confidential Clerk*, by T. S. Eliot.

Are the places in which the acts of this play are set of any significance? If so, how will the producer bring their significance to the audience?

CHAPTER XII

Rehearsals

NOW consider the planning of rehearsals of Barrie's
Dear Brutus. Compare the construction of Act I with
that of Act II. Act II consists of a series of duologues in this
order—Matey and Lady Caroline, Mabel and Purdie, and
Dearth and Margaret. Joanna and Coade intrude upon
Matey and Lady Caroline, Joanna lurks in the background
of the flirtation between Mabel and Purdie, and Coade and
Mrs. Dearth interrupt the delightful episode between Margaret and her father. But, in the main, this act is a sequence
of separate and independent duologues. On the other hand,
Act I opens with all the women characters, except Margaret,
on the stage, and they are soon followed by all the men.
The close of the act also involves the whole cast. In the
middle of this act, moreover, there are two very interesting
and important duologues—one between Purdie and Joanna,
interrupted by Mabel, another between Dearth and Mrs.
Dearth, with a piquant introduction between Mrs. Dearth
and Joanna.

This analysis indicates the need for organization of, and
method during, rehearsals. The opening, and the end, of
Act I, can be rehearsed only if all the characters are present;
whereas Act II and the middle parts of Act I can be
rehearsed sectionally with two, or at most three, characters
present. Joanna, Mabel, and Purdie have much to rehearse
which in no way concerns the other characters; similarly,
Margaret and Dearth; Mrs. Dearth and her husband; Lady
Caroline and Matey. Each of these sets of characters can
rehearse without reference to the other characters, and the
importance of each of their separate duologues demands
separate treatment and careful rehearsal. It is, therefore,
important that certain rehearsals shall be entirely devoted
to these couples, when they alone should be asked to attend.

Further consideration of the nature of these duologues brings the conclusion that they will be difficult to rehearse unless each of the characters is familiar with the words to be spoken. The charming flirtation between Joanna and Purdie is almost impossible if their portrayers are holding books. Similarly, it is not possible for Dearth to manipulate his brushes and canvas until he has perfect knowledge of the words he has to speak. The rehearsals of these separate duologues are best postponed until the actors are practically word-perfect. Then attention can be given to the problems which each of these separate episodes holds for the producer and for the actors—problems of speech, gesture and movement, of emphasis and stress.

On the other hand, the opening and end of Act I have problems of position and movement that may be effectively rehearsed even though the actors have still to learn their words, and are thus compelled to carry books with them upon the stage. Indeed, it may be of considerable value for them to have their books at the early rehearsals so that they may mark positions and movements as they occur throughout the scene. With such a large number of characters on the stage, positions and individual movements are of considerable importance. The sooner they are clearly established and known, the sooner will the cast be able to concentrate its attention upon the problems of interpretation. Early rehearsals should be arranged solely to fix these positions and movements.

For such rehearsals, punctuality and regularity are essential. Often rehearsal-appointments are made by people who have no intention of keeping them. Unpunctuality is an intolerable form of conceit; only the most urgent business or ill-health should cause absence. Much time is wasted because irresponsible folk arrange to attend rehearsals without really considering the probability of their keeping their promise. Every character in the opening of this act is playing an important part in the scene's general development. For rehearsal, each character must be represented.

The printed copy of the play should be compared with the "Prompt" copy. The play prepared for the reader opens with all the women characters on the stage; the play in the theatre opens with an empty stage, dark, except for the moonlight in the garden, seen through a French window at the back. After a moment voices are heard "off," and then the ladies enter as indicated by dialogue which serves as an introduction to the play proper. This introduction is performed entirely in the dark. These characters move, or, as Barrie says, they grope their way into the room, and when the lights are switched on we see them in the positions necessary for the forward movement of the scene.

Barrie's fondness for openings that demand the closest attention to detailed acting have been noted in *Quality Street*. These openings are really difficult because they set the atmosphere in which the whole play is performed. Mystery and conspiracy are at once established by this introduction—if proper care is taken over the entrances and speeches of the five ladies. This introduction, because of its intense acting difficulty, is better left to a later stage, when the actresses are more familiar with their characters, and have become familiar with the play. It is best rehearsed when the words are known, and when time can be spent on producing the necessary effect for the appropriate opening. It is wise, therefore, to spend no time upon it during the early rehearsals, but to wait until later, when all the cast are anxious to put the finishing touches to the production.

It is said sometimes that a play should be rehearsed "straight through." In the early days it is important to proceed only in so far as the play itself progresses straight on. The development of scenes is rarely continuous in the strict sense. There are many breaks, twists, and turns. Dramatically, these are combined to give a sense of continuity. Rehearsal can well follow the construction of the scenes. Each part can be rehearsed separately, and later combined to produce the effect of logical continuity. Obviously it would be a waste of several persons' time to rehearse straight through Act I of *Dear Brutus*. To rehearse Lob's conversation with his flowers, or the duologues of Joanna and Purdie, or of Dearth and Mrs. Dearth, while the others look on, is to create an atmosphere of unrest and dissatisfaction amongst the cast, and not to serve the interest of the play. The positions and movements for the early part of the act having been established, it is better to turn to the end of it when every character is again on the stage.

Each rehearsal should have its definite purpose and specific work. Announce that at the first rehearsal positions for those parts of Act I in which the majority of the characters are on the stage will be fixed. Stress the importance of every one being present, and that work cannot begin until all are there. Stress, also, the fact that the positions and movements for the climax of the scene will be rehearsed. If at the end of the first rehearsal the task that has been set has been performed, a valuable piece of work will have been done. Further, the cast will have gained confidence that when they are called for rehearsal they will be usefully employed.

To achieve these ends, the producer must attend the rehearsal prepared with stage plots and carefully worked out positions and movements. A small plan of the stage, drawn to scale, is valuable. It should indicate clearly the exact position of each piece of furniture, and, if possible, its respective size. Actors should be aware of the space in which they are to move, especially when there are several characters on the stage at one time. In addition, the producer should have ready a list of stage and hand properties necessary for the scene and have them, or equivalents, at the first rehearsal.

In the first act of *Dear Brutus*, Mrs. Dearth hands Matey a telegraphic message which she wishes him to send, and which she invites him to read. The movements of Matey are intimately concerned with this telegram. It is, therefore, useful to have a paper to pass from Mrs. Dearth to Matey. Similarly, when Matey returns the rings taken from the rooms of the various ladies, he should have objects to take from his pockets to hand to the particular ladies. Timing is important. Timed appropriately, this incident is good comedy; if it is done too hurriedly or too slowly, either it will bore the audience or completely misfire. Movement and detail can be rehearsed at the first rehearsal; knowledge of the lines is not an essential.

Perhaps two rehearsals can well be spent on movements for the first act with all the cast present. Even at this early stage in rehearsals attention can advantageously be directed to the climax of the scene. Besides getting positions and movements right, insistence on stressing the climax is of great value. The climax is the goal. Actors should always be aware of it. A producer should do his utmost to keep this moment in the minds of his cast. I have found that the surest way of getting the co-operation of those playing the parts is to let them know from the first the purpose I have had in mind.

At rehearsals of the separate duologues stress the importance of knowing the words. Expect the players to come to these rehearsals with a working knowledge of the words and prepared to rehearse without books. If in these duologues hand properties are needed, see that they are ready for use. Lob must have something to represent his flowers. Dearth must have his cigar, his paints, canvas, and easel. But at the first rehearsal of these episodes do not spend too much time on the manipulation of hand properties. At this stage it will, perhaps, be sufficient if it is clearly indicated that these properties have to be manipulated with due regard to correct timing and apparent spontaneity.

The value of rehearsals when only two or three characters are present cannot be over-stressed. At a rehearsal arranged for Joanna, Mabel, and Purdie the whole time can be devoted to their lovely flirtations! Their scenes are not long, and in two or three hours it is possible to go over them many times, giving attention to every detail of meaning, gesture, and expression.

Let me digress for one moment. Consider a great cricketer

or tennis player—Bradman or Perry. These players practise even after they have mastered the strokes upon which their prowess depends. Indeed, the important practice is that which follows the mastery of the strokes. So it should be with players. One of the tasks in rehearsal is to find a way for interpretation, the second—and perhaps even more important—is to rehearse that way when found.

This is a factor that amateurs frequently neglect. Producers should let players know when they are doing their parts well. When a particular scene is played excellently the producer should comment to that effect, and invite the players to repeat it. Not only does this encourage them and give them confidence, but it also establishes this way of performance and leads to confident and seemingly natural and spontaneous performance. It is part of the producer's business to assist the players to find a way to interpret character and to reveal the meaning of the text. By suggestion, by discussion, and even, where necessary, by demonstration, the producer must assist all those taking part. Beginners in the art of acting must frequently be shown how to interpret their parts. Sometimes the technique of speech and gesture is best taught by example.

Later it is important to rehearse the play straight through. Announce the time for starting and get agreement upon this. At the first rehearsal of this type, stress the fact that—no matter what mistakes are made—the intention is to go right through the play without any repetitions or interruptions of any kind. At such a rehearsal the producer will make notes of all the parts that are well done as well as of those that are badly done. He will especially take notice of the various climaxes and other important moments. After rehearsal he will make detailed comments, and, if there is time, some parts of the play will be gone over again. In any case, a special rehearsal, or rehearsals, will be called for the specific purpose of going over weak parts. A rehearsal of this kind has the special value of letting both the producer and the cast know what parts will need the greatest attention during the time available for the subsequent rehearsals.

In amateur productions the climaxes of the various scenes, and also that of the play itself, are often not sufficiently stressed or held. For this reason at least one rehearsal should be held for these particular moments to be specifically rehearsed. At this rehearsal the whole time should be devoted to these moments. Great care should be taken with the action that leads up to the climax, and also with the way in which the climax is to be held and stressed. It is no use merely talking about the climax; it is necessary for it to be rehearsed again and again so that this moment of the play is impressed upon the minds of the audience.

Act III of *Pygmalion* is particularly interesting—and difficult—because there are several moments at which excitement is aroused to an exceptional degree. Think of the moment when Eliza Doolittle makes her exit. This scene can easily break down at this point unless those left on the stage retain the interest of the audience. It should be remembered by those taking part that Eliza's exit is as sensational to them as it is to the audience. They may not respond to it in the same manner. Nevertheless, they are just as astonished and must, within the limits and scope of their individual characters, react to this astounding situation. Not only have they to do this, but they have to do it in spite of the audience. The laughter of the audience will be loud and long: there will be applause, but probably the audience will be indifferent to the artistic needs for continuity. Their excitement will arouse them to an outburst of enthusiastic approval. The play will be forgotten in their appreciation of that which they have just witnessed. The actors must rehearse for the transition back to the play. Shaw has carefully arranged for this reaction. With deft strokes he has given the players opportunities to reclaim the divided attention of the audience. The characters take some time to get over the shock, then silence is broken by Mrs. Eynesford Hill. The timing of this silence, as well as the acting of each individual character, must receive very careful rehearsal.

By-play also demands careful attention at rehearsal. Consider the Letter Scene in *Twelfth Night*. Malvolio finds the letter that is supposed to be from the Lady Olivia while the chief conspirators are watching behind the box-hedge. The scene must be carefully prepared and rehearsed. The producer must decide the points in the scene where the conspirators are seen above the hedge, and where they deliberately hide from Malvolio. The script of each of these must be marked with the instructions of their behaviour, and the scene must be rehearsed until all the movements seem to be the spontaneous result of the natural actions of all on the stage.

Whenever by-play is introduced into a scene it must be rehearsed until it has the appearance of being an essential development of the scene itself, and not merely something that has been put in for the sake of effect. Unless such actions have this appearance they should not be used. Time is well spent, even though there is much repetition, if at the end everything seems to be natural and spontaneous. Do not be afraid of constant repetition.

There are moments in every play that depend on perfect movement and timing. Such moments have to be persistently rehearsed. An example that springs to mind is in Act II of *Quality Street*, when Miss Phoebe, dressed in the wedding gown that Miss Susan has given her, is dancing to the music of the band playing outside. Miss Phoebe is wildly excited. As she whirls round the room she is oblivious to everything but her own thoughts. She hears Patty and her sister Susan speak, but she seems not to hear what they say.

On and on she dances until Captain Brown enters, causing her to stop abruptly. This dance interprets, in a way that words cannot, the conflicting emotions under which Phoebe is suffering. It must be rehearsed until it reveals the crescendo of rising emotion and elation, and timed so that Phoebe may be pulled up in the exact position required, and at the exact moment when she hears Captain Brown speak. The dance must appear to stop because Phoebe hears Captain Brown speak, and not because instructions have been given to that effect. The task here is to create the feeling that Phoebe dances as a result of her emotions, stimulated by the band, and that she stops because of the bewilderment from which she suffers when she hears Valentine Brown's voice.

Another moment that repays the utmost care is in Act IV when Valentine Brown pretends to wrap up in blankets a Miss Livy who is not there, and then calmly assists this non-existent young lady from the room. This is a charming piece of miming. Well done, it is theatrically most effective; carelessly done, stupid and childish.

It is perhaps unfortunate that rarely can amateurs have more than one dress rehearsal—particularly when the play happens to be a costume play. It is amazing that amateurs play in strange costumes as well as they do when it is remembered that all their rehearsals have to be done in their own clothes.

The dress rehearsal should be for the purposes of going through the whole play, becoming used to costumes, getting lighting effects satisfactory, polishing up entrances and exits, and rehearsing any effects with which it has been impossible to deal at previous rehearsals. There should, of course, be as few of these as possible. I recall in this connexion a production of *Secrets*. It had not been possible to rehearse the shooting effects with proper revolvers and rifles. The business with these had to be left to the dress rehearsal. There had, however, been preparation and careful rehearsals. Although no weapons had been used, the actual firing had been worked into a precise drill in which several workers off stage took part. At the dress rehearsal the revolvers and rifles were used and fired in just the same way as boxes had been thumped at rehearsal. All had been timed and numbered. Everybody knew exactly what was going to be done. The dress rehearsal was used to substitute rifles and revolvers for the drill previously rehearsed.

As far as possible a dress rehearsal should be treated as a performance. The curtain should be raised and lowered as at the actual performance. The stage should be set and properties arranged as they will be for the performance. The prompter should be in his place. And now just one word about the prompter's duties.

He is in the theatre, at the side of the stage, because it is always possible that a player may forget the words. He is there to assist a player who cannot remember. It is his duty immediately to speak the forgotten words in a voice that will be audible to those on the stage. The prompter must be audible and alert. He must follow every word that is spoken and be able to sense when a player is in need of prompting. It is annoying to receive a prompt when it is not wanted and distressing not to receive a prompt when it is needed. For these reasons it is necessary for the prompter to attend rehearsals, so that he may have knowledge of the general method of production, the general speed of the various scenes, and the pauses that the players will make. It is well for him to have his own copy of the play and to mark passages which, at rehearsal, cause players trouble and passages which are taken at a slow pace; also places where the players deliberately pause for effect. A good prompter gives confidence to those on the stage.

In connexion with prompting I offer a word of advice to players. If words are forgotten, stand still and listen for the prompter's voice. It is far better to make just a slight pause so that the words from the prompter can be caught than to muddle along, making up words.

SUMMARY

1. **Organization of and method at rehearsals.**
2. **Full rehearsals and sectional rehearsals.**
3. **Knowledge of words and rehearsals.**
4. **Rehearsals for fixing positions and movements.**
5. **Each rehearsal should have its definite purpose and specific work.**
6. **Stage plots and properties.**
7. **The importance of climax.**

8. Rehearsing right through the play.
9. Special rehearsals for the stressing of climaxes.
10. The rehearsing of by-play.
11. Rehearsal of moments demanding special attention to movement and timing.
12. Dress rehearsals.
13. The prompter.

CHAPTER XIII

Choosing a Play

MANY years ago a friend felt the urge to produce plays. He wanted to do this just as another person wishes to play the piano or to speak a foreign language. He did not think he had any very great gift for the task, or that he would succeed better than other persons. He just wanted to direct the performance of a play, to put a play on the stage, and to get it acted as he thought it should be acted.

It was neither his wish nor his intention to produce just *any* play. No, he knew definitely the plays he wanted to produce. He wanted to produce some of the plays of Shakespeare and of Sheridan. Particularly he wanted to produce *The Merchant of Venice* and *Twelfth Night* because they meant much to him.

He gathered together a cast. Some of the players were experienced and good, others were beginners of whose ability he knew nothing. The plays were rehearsed and performances were given. During rehearsals he found time to refer to other plays, especially to those he was eager to produce. He made it his business to work up enthusiasm for these, and did his utmost to make his cast as eager as he was to rehearse and perform them. During the rehearsals of *Twelfth Night*, the members of the cast were saying how jolly it would be to do *The School for Scandal*, and while that was being rehearsed they were suggesting it would be great fun to do another Shakespeare play, and asking: Why not *The Taming of the Shrew*? Always the players were being led towards the next play he intended to do.

After a time he wanted to direct the plays of Pinero, Wilde, Shaw, Barrie, and several other playwrights. For many years he produced plays with this group of players and never in all that time did the choice of play present any real problems.

Two other producers I have known intimately have been eager to produce only Shakespearian plays. For many years they have produced little else. Their success has been cutstanding. For them the task of choosing a play has been limited to the order in which they would do the plays of Shakespeare.

At a committee meeting where the choice of a play is discussed there is often difficulty in getting unanimity of opinion. Everybody has excellent reasons why this play should be rejected; why that one should be selected. But rarely is there agreement. My advice to all dramatic societies is: Elect your producer and leave the choice of the play to him (or her).

Frequently one is asked what plays are suitable for amateurs. My reply is—any good play. The only plays amateurs should avoid are bad ones. Mr. Sean O'Casey broadcast that it was better for amateurs to do good plays badly than bad plays well. I see no reason why anybody should want to perform bad plays! Amateurs and students, especially, should give their attention to good plays only. It is a waste of time and energy to rehearse bad plays, and an insult to friends to ask them to sit for three hours watching the performance of such plays. And why pay royalties to the author of a bad play when there are so many good ones?

It is sometimes urged that amateurs should restrict themselves to plays within the scope of their abilities. Were we to accept this as a criterion for the choice of play, I fear there would be rigid limitation. Surely it is to the professional player that this advice should be given, not to the amateur? No play can be too good for the amateur or for his audience. Good plays provide interest throughout rehearsals for those who take part, and give interest to an audience during performance.

The point is sometimes made that modern drama is more readily understood and more easily interpreted because the characters are more nearly like the players themselves, and because the themes are closer to contemporaneous conditions. It is also stated that because the plays of Shakespeare reach the highest pinnacle of dramatic art they are, therefore, the most difficult to perform. Neither statement is accurate. Experience illustrates that a number of modern plays, by reason of their psychological and sociological implications, are extremely difficult for all but the best players, while interesting performances of some of Shakespeare's comedies have been given by beginners in the art of acting. Experience also tends to illustrate that greater progress in the acquisition of skill in acting is made by practice in Shakespearian plays than in those of any other dramatist.

These contentions bring to mind the work of a society in which I was much interested a few years ago. It had given several stimulating performances of Shakespeare's plays and was eager to present a modern play. Shaw's *You Never Can Tell* was chosen, and the players were looking forward to an easier and—some said—a more interesting time. They set to work in high spirits, but as the date of the performance drew near, they realized that they were getting nothing from the play. They could make little of the characters, and the play would not move smoothly. In desperation they determined to rehearse every evening, all Saturday afternoon, and on Sunday. This they did for a month and in the end they gave a tolerably good performance. They certainly enjoyed their work, and they have never regretted the time spent on the self-appointed task. But they have not since imagined that a modern work is necessarily simpler to understand or to interpret than one of Shakespeare's plays.

Dramatic presentation is at once a most alluring and intense form of literary experience, especially for adolescents. For this reason alone it is important that leaders of amateur and student groups should choose only the best plays for rehearsal and performance.

Plays in which the characters are clearly drawn, and which depend for their interest upon human conflict, are generally more suitable than those in which incident forms the basis of dramatic interest. These provide the player with something tangible for him to work at and to interpret. He has an enormous field from which to choose, and, provided choice of play is not confused with other problems, there should be little difficulty in making a selection from the works of the great dramatists from Shakespeare's time to our own.

Probably the interest in drama and the theatre has never been greater than it is to-day. It is almost true to say that wherever a number of people are gathered together, either to live or to work, there has emerged a group to rehearse and perform plays. Amateur players were never more numerous or more versatile than at the present time.

One very important result of this development of interest in dramatic presentation has been the enormous increase in the popularity of the one-act play. Authors of repute are turning their attention to this form of dramatic expression, and there are excellent little plays for the amateur. For schools and groups where it is necessary to provide a fairly large number of people with work, these short plays are of considerable value, and some very interesting triple bills can be arranged by making a careful selection.

It should, however, be observed that for every good one-act play that is published there are many bad ones. Writers of little distinction turn their pens to this profitable source of income, with a result that there are one-act plays the only merit of which is that they are written in dialogue. Avoid these worthless things and spend time only on those plays that have real dramatic merit.

As a change from the performances of one-act plays groups should consider giving a series of excerpts from full-length plays. Many scenes from the plays of both Shakespeare and modern dramatists are understandable on their own account, without reference to the play from which they are taken. Such scenes make excellent programmes for the public, and study and rehearsal of them do much to solve the difficult problem of providing work for a number of people. Additional value is that in this way knowledge and experience of that which is best in drama are gained by those taking part.

Perhaps the greatest value of the amateur movement lies in the experience of literature and life that is obtained by all concerned. For the majority it is an experience of life that is drawn from the study and performance of a play. Experience of life is often confined to the narrow circle of the daily round. The study of drama becomes an experience of life, affording new emotions, new ideas, fresh knowledge of people, things, movements, and social conditions. Herein lie the value of amateur societies to its own members, and the reason why it is of the greatest importance to perform only the best plays.

In the glossary I have given a list of plays that I believe worthy of study and of production. The list is incomplete, but it will be useful to those who are in search of a play. Naturally, some of these plays are more difficult than others; some present staging difficulties; others are rendered difficult because of certain complex characters. The majority, however, can be interestingly interpreted by keen players who are willing to rehearse seriously.

In addition to the titles of plays by well-known British dramatists, I have given a few by foreign authors. Most of these are well known to British audiences, and some of them have already exerted considerable influence upon our own drama and our own theatre. A season devoted to such plays would not be wasted. Many of them are reasonably simple, and even such difficult ones as *The Insect Play* and *Mourning Becomes Electra* are worthy of serious consideration. I have seen interesting performances of *The Insect Play* by amateurs.

For those who have learned how to speak, who are sensitive to fine language, and are not afraid of strenuous rehearsals, there are beautiful verse plays, both one-act and full-length. One of these, in blank verse, is *Will Shakespeare*, by Clemence Dane. This play was first acted at the Shaftesbury Theatre in 1921 and unfortunately did not prove a "box-office" draw. Yet it deserved to be. It is an excellent play, and for the amateur, not controlled in his choice by considerations that must affect the professional, one that should prove attractive. Its staging is simple, little furniture is required, and its lighting problems are easily overcome. Its interpretation depends entirely upon speech, movement, and characterization. The characters are clearly drawn, and are splendid acting parts. In addition, there is a large crowd, representing "shadows" of the characters from Shakespeare's plays. These "shadows" have a fascinating and important part in the first act and provide interesting work for a large number of people. Certainly the play is difficult, but for those who rehearse it with proper seriousness it provides an unforgettable experience.

In recent years a most interesting experiment in playwriting has been made by our leading poets. The leader of this movement was W. B. Yeats, the great Irish poet and dramatist. His *Four Plays for Dancers* attain a delightful balance between the literary qualities of language and the dramatic qualities of fine speech, rhythmic movement, and characterization. The lyric verse is beautiful, requiring the finest and most sensitive speech for its interpretation, while the mythological heroes of the drama call for specialized movement and gesture in the creation of a true illusion of their character quality.

These plays are not written for performance in the ordinary commercial theatre, and they will, perhaps, be of no interest to those who can think of a play only in terms of footlights, grease paints, and painted scenery. But for the student, and for all who are seriously interested in the art of the theatre and the art of acting, they provide a most fascinating study.

They are written for performance in a large drawing-room or very small hall, and before an audience of not more than fifty. For performance they demand players with special ability in speech and movement, and an audience that cares for fine lyrical poetry. But surely these demands should not surprise. The former demand is one that should be made for the interpretation of any kind of play, and the latter is but the expressed acceptance of a normal condition. The Old Vic has its patrons: so have the Lyceum and the Gaiety.

These little plays do not lack dramatic merit because they would prove unacceptable in a West End theatre, or because they would fail to interest a popular audience. Their dramatic quality is completely vindicated by the delight, even thrill, which they are capable of giving to a selected audience when they are sympathetically interpreted by appropriately skilled players.

None of the appurtenances usually associated with a theatre is required, not even a proscenium curtain. But, while the impermanent, and sometimes meretricious, qualities of the theatre are dispensed with, the permanent and essential qualities of speech, movement, and gesture are preserved as the vehicles of dramatic expression. For Yeats the theatre had to be "the ancient theatre that can be made by unrolling a carpet or marking out a place with a stick, or setting a screen against a wall." In such a theatre the imagination is not baulked by a striving after reality, but remains free for the reception of any illusion the dramatist may wish to create.

For these plays no scenery is necessary, for the scene of each play is beautifully described to the audience by a musician. Here is the description of the scene for *The Only Jealousy of Emer*—

> I call before the eyes a roof
> With cross-beams darkened by smoke:
> A fisher's net hangs from a beam,
> A long oar lies against the wall.
> I call up a poor fisher's house:
> A man lies dead or swooning,
> That amorous man,
> That amorous, violent man, renowned Cuchulain,
> Queen Emer at his side.

In imagination we visualize the "fisher's house" before us and see Emer by the side of the dead or swooning Cuchulain.

The characters are heroic figures taken from Celtic mythology. They are made to wear very beautiful costumes, and masks specially designed to create an illusion of each specific character. These masks are in no way eccentric; on the contrary, they readily help one to believe in a legendary world in which these semi-supernatural characters live and move. But the visual attraction of the masks and the close proximity of the audience impose upon the player a definite approach to interpretation.

Yeats was ever conscious that drama is something tha tis shown and not that which is merely spoken about, and the masks compel the player to concentrate attention upon finding appropriate movement and gesture for the play's interpretation. The visual attractiveness of the masks may easily absorb the attention of the audience. Their fixed expression may haunt the imagination until they become things of horror instead of beauty. Thus movement becomes an imperative condition of performance. Movement of the entire body must provide the expression demanded by the language spoken, and by the mythological characters of the story.

Yeats invented a picturesque method of opening these plays. For the usual rising of the curtain he introduces a practical device of curtain bearing and curtain folding. The stage is just a space before a wall of any room, or a patterned screen. Musicians enter. One of them is carrying a long, folded cloth. They walk to the middle of the stage and towards the front, then two of the musicians unfold the curtain, singing as they do so. While the curtain is across the acting space, the stage is set as required by the conditions of the play. The curtain is then folded and carried to one side of the stage.

Gordon Bottomley in his plays developed this idea of curtain bearers by introducing a large chorus which itself curtains the stage while it is being prepared for action and which is then interwoven into the action to form an integral part of the play.

In *The Singing Sands* the stage is described as

A vacant space. A chorus of WAVES enter. Eight or more women dressed in clinging green, with large sweeping sleeves range themselves across the front of the space.

The chorus speaks and moves rhythmically to suggest waves, while behind it is placed the scenic representation of the mouth of a cave and some rocks. Finally, the waves open out and group about the space to discover to the audience the characters of the play entering between the rocks and moving towards the mouth of the cave. In one performance of this play by a group of students the chorus itself took up positions to represent symbolically the mouth of the cave. This was found to be entirely effective.

The Singing Sands and *Ardvorlich's Wife* are two plays by Gordon Bottomley that are of considerable value and interest to groups of students studying the drama. Their interpretation demands a simple, direct speech, and a careful study of movement. The choruses provide a study of the utmost value. They are not merely introductions to the play and its characters or commentaries upon the action; they are dramatic, and provide balance and poise in the development of the drama. For their vocalization the greatest care and control are required; control of pitch, tone, speed, rhythm, emphasis, and strength. All taking part must be conscious of the effects desired and the means to obtain them. The effort to obtain the required dramatic significance of the chorus is a most valuable experiment and experience.

To this practice in vocalization must be added movement, and, what is of the utmost importance, a careful study of repose. Movement and repose are essential qualities of acting. The chorus must acquire graceful and rhythmic movement. It is equally necessary for those taking part to attain a high degree of control in repose, for on the stage it is ever providing, as it were, a background to the principal characters when it is not taking an active part in the play's development.

Perhaps the most important contributions to modern verse drama are the two great plays by T. S. Eliot: *The Rock*, and *Murder in the Cathedral*. Both illustrate the power of verse as a vehicle of dramatic expression, and make considerable use of the chorus. *Murder in the Cathedral* had a wonderful success in the commercial theatre. It should prove equally successful in the non-commercial theatre.

For students of speech and of acting no plays provide greater opportunities than verse plays, and, although they are not nearly so prolific as are prose plays, those that we have are very beautiful. The verse plays of W. H. Auden and Christopher Isherwood, Clifford Bax, Laurence Binyon, Gordon Bottomley, and W. B. Yeats are delightful to rehearse and to play, and experience tends to show that audiences are both interested and thrilled by them.

SUMMARY

1. **The urge to produce.**
2. **The difficulty of securing unanimity in the choice of play.**
3. **Elect your producer and leave the choice of play to him.**
4. **Any good play is suitable. The only plays amateurs should avoid are bad ones.**
5. **Modern plays are not necessarily easier to understand or to interpret than are Shakespeare's plays.**
6. **Plays depending for their interest on human conflict are generally more suitable than those in which incident forms the basis of dramatic interest.**
7. **The growth of the one-act play.**
8. **Excerpts from full-length plays make excellent programmes.**
9. **Perhaps the amateur movement's greatest value lies in the experience of literature and life that is gained by all taking part.**
10. **A season devoted to the plays of foreign authors is not wasted.**
11. *Will Shakespeare*, **by Clemence Dane.**
12. **W. B. Yeats and the** *Four Plays for Dancers.*
13. **Curtain bearing and curtain folding.**

14. Gordon Bottomley and his use of the chorus.
15. The value of the chorus in studying speech and movement.
16. *Murder in the Cathedral*, by T. S. Eliot.
17. W. H. Auden and Christopher Isherwood, Clifford Bax, Laurence Binyon, Gordon Bottomley, and W. B. Yeats.

A GLOSSARY OF PLAYS

PLAYS SUITABLE FOR YOUNG PEOPLE UNDER THE AGE OF 15 YEARS

Clifford Bax:	*Old King Cole.*
Clemence Dane:	*Shivering Shocks.*
John Drinkwater:	*Robin Hood and the Pedlar.*
A. P. Herbert:	*Fat King Melon.*
Maurice Maeterlinck:	*The Blue Bird.* Act II, Scene 2.
Miles Malleson:	*Paddly Pools.*
	Michael.
A. A. Milne:	*Make Believe.*
Hermon Ould:	*The Discovery.*
Shakespeare:	*A Midsummer Night's Dream.*
	The Merchant of Venice.
	Twelfth Night.
	As You Like It.
	Macbeth.
	Julius Caesar.
Ethel Sidgwick:	*The Rose and the Ring.*
Evelyn Smith:	*The Swineherd.*
	Alice in Wonderland.
	A Christmas Carol.
Rosalind Vallance:	*Pandora's Box.*

PLAYS SUITABLE FOR YOUNG PEOPLE UNDER THE AGE OF 18 YEARS

Many of the foregoing.

Maurice Baring:	*Catherine Parr.*
	The Rehearsal.
Sir James Barrie:	*Quality Street.*
	The Admirable Crichton.
	A Kiss for Cinderella.
	The Old Lady Shows her Medals.
Clifford Bax:	*The Poetasters of Ispahan.*
	The Cloak.
Laurence Binyon:	*Sophro the Wise.*
Harold Brighouse:	*Followers.*
Olive Conway:	*Becky Sharp.*
Walter de la Mare:	*Crossings.*
Thomas Dekker:	*The Shoemaker's Holiday.*
John Drinkwater:	$X = 0.$
Lord Dunsany:	*The Golden Doom.*
	A Night at an Inn.

Oliver Goldsmith:	*She Stoops to Conquer.*
	The Good-natured Man.
Stanley Houghton:	*The Dear Departed.*
Laurence Housman and	
Harley Granville-Barker:	*Prunella.*
Norman McKinnell:	*The Bishop's Candlesticks.*
Margaret Macnamara:	*Elizabeth Refuses.*
Allan Monkhouse:	*The Grand Cham's Diamond.*
Shakespeare:	Those previously given and:
	Henry IV, Part 1.
	Henry V.
	Richard II.
	Romeo and Juliet.
Sheridan:	*The Rivals.*
	The Critic.
F. Sladen-Smith:	*The Invisible Duke.*
Evelyn Smith:	*Comus.*
	The Mill on the Floss.
	Nicholas Nickleby.
Sophocles:	*Antigone.*
Mona Swann:	*Saul and David.*
Dan Totheroh:	*The Stolen Prince.*
W. B. Yeats:	*Land of Heart's Desire.*
	The Pot of Broth.

PLAYS SUITABLE FOR PEOPLE OVER 18 YEARS OF AGE

Most of the plays already given are suitable for study and performance by adults.

Anthony Armstrong:	*Ten Minute Alibi.*
J. L. Balderston:	*Berkeley Square.*
Harley Granville-Barker:	*The Voysey Inheritance.*
	Waste.
	The Madras House.
Sir James Barrie:	*Quality Street.*
	The Admirable Crichton.
	Alice Sit-by-the-Fire.
	Dear Brutus.
	Mary Rose.
	The Professor's Love Story.
	A Kiss for Cinderella.
Clifford Bax:	*The Rose without a Thorn.*
	The Venetian.

Beaumont and Fletcher:	*The Knight of the Burning Pestle.*
Arnold Bennett:	*Milestones.*
	The Great Adventure.
Reginald Berkeley:	*The Lady with a Lamp.*
Rudolf Besier:	*Secrets.*
	The Barretts of Wimpole Street.
James Bridie:	*Tobias and the Angel.*
	The Sleeping Clergyman.
Harold Brighouse:	*Hobson's Choice.*
Paul V. Carroll:	*Shadow and Substance.*
Noel Coward:	*The Young Idea.*
	Hay Fever.
Agatha Christie:	*Ten Little Niggers.*
	The Mouse Trap.
	The Hollow.
Dorothy and Campbell Christie:	*Carrington, V.C.*
Clemence Dane:	*Will Shakespeare.*
	A Bill of Divorcement.
	Wild Decembers.
Gordon Daviot:	*Richard of Bordeaux.*
John Dighton:	*The Happiest Days of Your Life.*
John Drinkwater:	*Abraham Lincoln.*
	Bird in Hand.
	Robert E. Lee.
	Mary Stuart.
	Oliver Cromwell.
John Van Druten:	*London Wall.*
	The Distaff Side.
Ashley Dukes:	*The Man with a Load of Mischief.*
	Such Men are Dangerous.
Lord Dunsany:	*If.*
St. John Ervine:	*The Ship.*
	The First Mrs. Fraser.
	The Lady of Belmont.
	Jane Clegg.
	Mixed Marriage.
	John Ferguson.
	Robert's Wife.
	People of our Class.
Bernard Fagan:	*And So to Bed.*
John Galsworthy:	*The Silver Box.*
	The Skin Game.
	Old English.
	Loyalties.

John Galsworthy:	*Escape.*
	Justice.
	The Roof.
Oliver Goldsmith:	*She Stoops to Conquer.*
	The Good-natured Man.
Graham Greene:	*The Living Room.*
Merton Hodge:	*The Wind and the Rain.*
	The Island.
Monckton Hoffe:	*Many Waters.*
Laurence Housman and	*Prunella.*
Harley Granville-Barker	
N. C. Hunter:	*Waters of the Moon.*
Denis Johnston:	*The Moon in Yellow River.*
Henry A. Jones:	*The Hypocrites.*
	The Liars.
	Mrs. Dane's Defence.
Edward Knoblock:	*My Lady's Dress.*
Benn W. Levy:	*Mrs. Moonlight.*
Frederick Lonsdale:	*The Last of Mrs. Cheyney.*
	The High Road.
Norman MacOwan:	*Glorious Morning.*
John Masefield:	*The Tragedy of Nan.*
	Pompey the Great.
J. C. Masterman:	*Marshal Ney.*
Somerset Maugham:	*The Land of Promise.*
	Caesar's Wife.
	The Circle.
	East of Suez.
	For Services Rendered.
A. A. Milne:	*The Romantic Age.*
	Mr. Pim Passes By.
	The Great Broxopp.
	The Dover Road.
	The Truth About Blayds.
	Success.
Charles Morgan:	*The River Line.*
	The Burning Glass.
	The Flashing Stream.
C. K. Munro:	*At Mrs. Beam's.*
Ivor Novello:	*The Truth Game.*
Sean O'Casey:	*Juno and the Paycock.*
	The Plough and the Stars.
Eden Phillpotts.	*The Farmer's Wife.*
	Yellow Sands.

Sir Arthur Pinero:	*Trelawney of the Wells.*
	The Second Mrs. Tanqueray.
	His House in Order.
J. B. Priestley:	*Dangerous Corner.*
	Laburnum Grove.
	The Linden Tree
	An Inspector Calls.
	They Came to a City.
	Time and the Conways.
	When We are Married.
Terence Rattigan:	*The Browning Version.*
	The Winslow Boy.
	The Deep Blue Sea.
	The Sleeping Prince.
A. Ridley:	*The Ghost Train.*
T. W. Robertson:	*Caste.*
Lennox Robinson:	*The White headed Boy.*
Elsie T. Schauffler:	*Parnell.*
Mordaunt Shairp:	*The Crime at Blossom's.*
George Bernard Shaw:	*Arms and the Man*
	Candida.
	You Never Can Tell.
	Caesar and Cleopatra.
	Androcles and the Lion.
	Pygmalion.
	Man and Superman.
	Heartbreak House.
	Saint Joan.
Sheridan:	*The School for Scandal.*
	The Rivals.
R. C. Sherriff:	*Journey's End.*
Dodie Smith:	*Service.*
	Call it a Day.
	Dear Octopus.
Aimée and Philip Stuart:	*Nine Till Six.*
Peter Ustinov:	*The Love of Four Colonels.*
Sutton Vane:	*Outward Bound.*
Frank Vosper:	*Murder on the Second Floor.*
Oscar Wilde:	*Lady Windermere's Fan.*
	The Importance of Being Earnest.
Emlyn Williams:	*A Murder Has Been Arranged.*
	The Late Christopher Bean.
	The Corn is Green.
Any of Shakespeare's plays.	

INTERESTING ONE-ACT PLAYS

Sir James Barrie:	*Rosalind.*
	The Will.
	The Twelve Pound Look.
	Shall We Join the Ladies?
Mark Bevan:	*Nor Care Beyond Today.*
Harold Brighouse:	*Followers.*
	The Stoker.
	The Dye-Hard.
	Smoke Screens.
Yves Cabrol:	*The Neighbours.*
Lord Dunsany:	*A Night at an Inn.*
J. O. Francis:	*The Poacher.*
John Galsworthy:	*The Little Man.*
Lady Gregory:	*The Workhouse Ward.*
L. Hines and F. King:	*Bamboo.*
Stanley Houghton:	*The Dear Departed.*
Philip Johnson:	*The Lovely Miracle.*
	The Spinsters of Lushe.
Margaret Macnamara:	*Elizabeth Refuses.*
A. A. Milne:	*The Boy Comes Home.*
	The Man in the Bowler Hat.
Josephina Niggli:	*Sunday Costs 5 Pesos.*
T. B. Morris:	*Swan-Song.*
Eugene O'Neill:	*Where the Cross is Made.*
Edward Percy:	*Women at War.*
H. F. Rubinstein:	*The Theatre.*
Hans Sachs:	*The Strolling Clerk from Paradise.*
(English by Philip Wayne)	
F. Sladen-Smith:	*The Poison Party.*
	The Invisible Duke.
Arthur Swinson:	*The Sword is Double Edged.*
J. M. Synge:	*The Shadow of the Glen.*
	Riders to the Sea.
W. St. John Tayleur:	*Reunion.*
Anton Chekhov:	*The Bear.*
	The Proposal.
Thornton Wilder:	*The Happy Journey.*
	Love and How to Cure it.

MODERN VERSE PLAYS

Clifford Bax:	*The Rose and the Cross.*
	The Cloak.

Clifford Bax:	*Prelude and Fugue.*
	Square Pegs.
	The Unknown Hand.
Rudolf Besier:	*The Virgin Goddess.*
Laurence Binyon:	*Sophro the Wise.*
	Love in the Desert.
Gordon Bottomley:	*King Lear's Wife.*
	Gruach.
	The Singing Sands.
	Ardvorlich's Wife.
	A Parting.
	The Return.
John Brandane:	*Man of Uz.*
Robert Bridges:	*Achilles in Scyros.*
Clemence Dane:	*Will Shakespeare.*
John Drinkwater:	*The Storm.*
	X = 0.
	Cophetua.
T. S. Eliot:	*The Cocktail Party.*
	The Confidential Clerk.
	The Rock.
	Murder in the Cathedral.
Christopher Fry:	*The Lady's not for Burning.*
	Venus Observed.
	A Phoenix Too Frequent.
John Masefield:	*Tristan and Isolt.*
	A King's Daughter.
	End and Beginning.
	Easter.
	Good Friday.
	The Coming of Christ.
Stephen Phillips:	*Herod.*
	The Sin of David.
	Paola and Francesca.
W. B. Yeats:	*The Land of Heart's Desire.*
	The Countess Cathleen.
	The Four Plays for Dancers.
	(*a*) *At the Hawk's Well.*
	(*b*) *The Only Jealousy of Emer.*
	(*c*) *The Dreaming of the Bones.*
	(*d*) *Calvary.*

PLAYS FROM FOREIGN SOURCES

AMERICAN:

Maxwell Anderson:	*Winterset.*

Maxwell Anderson:	*The Masque of Kings.*
John Balderston:	*Berkeley Square.*
Marc Connelly:	*Green Pastures.*
George Kaufman:	*Dinner at Eight.*
Clifford Odets:	*Awake and Sing.*
	Paradise Lost.
	Golden Boy.
	Waiting for Lefty.
Eugene O'Neill:	*Anna Christie.*
	The Emperor Jones.
	The Hairy Ape.
	All God's Chillun Got Wings.
	Strange Interlude.
	Ah, Wilderness.
	Mourning Becomes Electra.
Elmer Rice:	*The Adding Machine.*
	Street Scene.
Dan Totheroh:	*Moor Born.*
	The Stolen Prince. (Short play.)

BELGIUM:

Maurice Maeterlinck:	*The Blue Bird.*
	Pelléas and Mélisande.
	The Burgomaster of Stilemonde.

CZECHOSLOVAKIA:

Karel Čapek:	*R.U.R.*
	The Insect Play.
	Power and Glory.

GERMANY:

| Christa Winsloe: | *Children in Uniform.* |

HUNGARY:

| F. Molnar: | *Liliom.* |

ITALY:

Pirandello:	*Six Characters in Search of an Author.*
	Henry IV.
	Right You Are.

RUSSIA:

| Chekhov: | *Three Sisters.* |
| | *The Cherry Orchard.* |

SCANDINAVIA:

Ibsen:	*The Doll's House.*
	An Enemy of the People.
	Pillars of Society.

Ibsen:	*The Wild Duck.*
	Rosmerholm.
	Hedda Gabler.
	Peer Gynt.
SPAIN:	
Sierra:	*The Cradle Song.*
	The Kingdom of God.
Quintero:	*A Hundred Years Old.*

INDEX